THE COMMUNITY OF EUROPE

THE COMMUNITY OF EUROPE

by

RICHARD MAYNE

Introduction by
JEAN MONNET

W · W · NORTON & COMPANY · INC ·
NEW YORK

To
MARGOT

TO THE READER

I FIND SOME difficulty in writing a preface for Richard Mayne's outstanding book because it contains such friendly references to myself. But its subject is such — and the importance of its subject is so great — that I feel bound, as well as privileged, to do so.

In it, I think, the reader will find what I have found: that it not only describes clearly and vividly at first hand the workings of the Common Market and the European Community, but puts them in their true setting. For [the Common Market is not a static creation; it is a new and dynamic phase in the development of our civilization. The essential characteristic of this new phase is that nations have now begun to accept that their problems are joint problems and cannot be settled by national measures only.] *pre-Jan., 1963*

The virtue of the Common Market is to use this realization creatively, by applying joint measures through common rules and institutions — the method which in other spheres is already acknowledged as the basis of civilized society.

The success of this new approach is already evident in the new relationship between European countries which for centuries have been locked in rivalry and strife. In turn, this new relationship is already transforming the international scene as a whole. Great Britain is debating membership in the European Community; the United States envisages partnership with it; even the Soviet Union shows signs of admitting its validity.

One day, perhaps, the new methods adopted in the Common

Market may be used to meet even broader challenges and to create even greater opportunities. The great merit of this book, in my opinion, is that it is the first to seize clearly upon the nature of this new dynamic, and to present it simply and forcefully in the context of rapidly moving events.

Jean Monnet

CONTENTS

PREFACE

THE TITLE OF this book is *The Community of Europe*: it is not a book about the Common Market only, and still less a tract urging that Britain join, or not join, the European Community. It is simply a brief history of a great movement.

In writing it, I have tried to avoid covering once again what is already the subject of so many excellent studies, and so much voluminous documentation, from other pens.

As an Englishman who has been involved in these questions for about a decade, and has worked on the European Community staff for the past six years, I find it almost impossible to feel detached, but I have tried to be objective. If a view from both sides of the fence is an impartial view, perhaps I have succeeded.

Finally, I should like to record my gratitude to the Commission of the European Economic Community for permission to write the present work, and to point out that all responsibility for the views and conclusions expressed here is entirely my own.

R. J. M.

Haamstede, 1962

CHAPTER I

THE EUROPEAN COMMUNITY—AN EMERGING PATTERN

MAPS CHANGE, BUT words remain the same. Today, the map of "Europe" that many of us remember from our schooldays is almost as archaic as the pages of an historical atlas showing the vanished frontiers of the Austro-Hungarian Empire. Three countries—Esthonia, Latvia, and Lithuania—have disappeared from it entirely. Germany is divided; and the *de facto* frontiers of the Soviet Union now include sizeable slices of Finland, East Prussia, Poland, Czechoslovakia, and Rumania. Even to the West of those frontiers, the so-called "Iron Curtain" crosses the continent from the Baltic to Greece: and any realistic account of postwar attempts to unite "Europe" must begin with the cardinal fact that the old Europe is already divided.

The subject of this book, therefore, is essentially Western Europe; but even here the old map is no longer reliable. It is not only that frontiers are being re-drawn—although Italy's Jugoslav border has been adjusted, the Saar has returned from France to Germany, and the Dutch have transformed the Zuider Zee into the Ijsselmeer, a vast salt lake. The new element is a gradual change in the nature of frontiers, and a corresponding change, not only in international relations, but also in the nature of the state itself.

This process is partly a response to the technological changes that have reduced distances, made possible mass production, and enormously increased men's means of mutual annihilation. As such, it can be observed everywhere, in the countries of Eastern

Europe as well as in the West, and in Latin America no less than in emergent Africa, where even nationalist independence movements seek common cause in "Panafrican" aspirations. Nevertheless, it is the countries of Western Europe that have most deliberately sought to transcend national barriers, not only in such international ventures as the Council of Europe, the Organization for European Economic Co-operation, Western European Union, and Benelux, but also—far more radically—in the construction by France, Germany, Italy and the three Benelux countries, of what has come to be known as "The European Community". It is this Community that the United Kingdom is now seeking to join.

Already, the crossing of frontiers in most regions of Western Europe is agreeably simple, whether one travels by air, by rail, or by road. A routine question from a bored customs officer, a rapid glance at a simple identity card, a perfunctory flourish of car insurance papers, and one enters another country: on occasion, driving on a motorway at night, I have even passed a frontier post without seeing it at all. The simplification of border formalities is one of the achievements of the Council of Europe, the O.E.E.C., and the United Nations' Economic Commission for Europe; but the aims of the European Community, although they embrace a smaller area, are very much more ambitious. They involve, indeed, the total elimination, not merely of frontier formalities, but of frontiers' economic effects.

The history of the European Community formally began more than ten years ago with the Schuman Plan for a European Coal and Steel Community (E.C.S.C.), and has continued with the European Economic Community (the Common Market) and the European Atomic Energy Community (Euratom). In these organizations, the Community countries have set themselves the task of gradually abolishing all national obstacles to the movement of goods, people, and capital throughout their combined territory; of establishing within it a single integrated economy under common rules and institutions; and of adopting a common policy—as well as a common external tariff—in their economic dealings with the rest of the world. Moreover, although the subject-matter of these endeavours may appear to be economic, their implications and objectives are openly political. Indeed, the Community countries are committed by Treaty to the achievement of an "ever closer union" that many Europeans see as the embryo of a future "United States of Europe".

This phrase, like most political slogans, has the double advantage of being at once spirited and imprecise: it affords verbal shelter for both the federalist lion and the internationalist lamb. For Jean Monnet, "the United States of Europe have already begun"—had begun, indeed, in 1955 when his book of that title was published. General de Gaulle, the advocate of *"l'Europe des Etats"*, who sees the Community institutions as purely technical machinery with limited aims, would hardly have agreed with him. The bulk of the Gaullist party, in fact, voted against ratification of the European Coal and Steel Community Treaty in December 1951. But even General de Gaulle has since looked forward to "an imposing confederation", and under his leadership France has scrupulously respected the legal provisions of the Community Treaties.

Similar scruples were shown in 1954 by Pierre Mendès-France, whose Government failed to secure French ratification of the Treaty to set up a European Defence Community (E.D.C.). After the *débâcle*, although no enthusiast for the existing European Coal and Steel Community, he was at pains to assure a Member of its Executive that since France had ratified the E.C.S.C. Treaty she would continue to honour her word. In Germany, the Social Democrats who had voted against the E.C.S.C. in 1952 became loyal and active members of its Common Assembly, and by 1957 were willing to vote for the Common Market and Euratom. In Italy, even the Nenni Socialists, who had opposed the E.C.S.C. in alliance with the

Communists, later voted in favour of Euratom and merely abstained from the vote on the Common Market. It may be significant, too, that during the 1961 general election in Belgium, the country whose economy has perhaps most to fear from integration with its neighbours, and in whose depressed coalmining area the E.C.S.C. is widely if unjustly blamed for the closure of uneconomic pits, no candidate other than the Communists denounced the European Community as such : opposition spokesmen preferred to attack the Government for its alleged failure to prepare the Belgian economy for the Common Market's impact.

Beyond the Common Market, moreover, all the Member Governments of the Community were party to the Bonn Declaration of July 18, 1961, whereby they decided "to give shape to the will for political union already implicit in the Treaties establishing the European Communities". Although the formula chosen was sufficiently vague to accommodate a variety of contrasting interpretations, the fact of the Declaration is itself significant; and those who professionally or otherwise get too deeply involved in day-to-day battles over its exegesis may risk not seeing the wood for the trees. In fact, the doctrinal and other disputes that chequer the Community's history are largely disagreements about the form of future unity rather than the calling into question of a general process to which all parties are more or less committed.

Not all Community citizens, of course, are fully aware of what is going on. Every democracy has its proportion of "Don't Knows". But in public life there is certainly a sense of general acquiescence : "Europe" is something of a shibboleth, an O.K.-word; and to be opposed to "European unity" is almost as unrespectable in the Community countries as it is eccentric in Great Britain to be against "international co-operation". Not long ago, a French Gaullist Minister, addressing a congress of teachers, was told by his audience that European integration was one of the few "causes" that nowadays inspired the young. In all the Community countries, moreover, "European" enthusiasm is encouraged both by political leaders and journalists—perhaps especially from the Catholic and Socialist parties—and by a swarming multiplicity of propagandist periodicals, associations, vested interests, and pressure groups. Of the latter, the most directly influential is the "Action Committee for the United States of Europe", headed by Jean Monnet and comprising representatives of all the chief non-Communist political parties and trade unions in the Community, which not only finance the Committee's activities but also in many cases consider themselves bound by its resolutions. There will be more to say of this, and of Monnet's rôle in European integration, on a later page.

There is nothing wholly far-fetched, therefore, in a map of Western Europe that shows the Community countries all in the same colour—although there is still much uncertainty about its shading. In many ways, these countries seem to be beginning to share a sense of solidarity and common purpose far more thoroughgoing than that which loosely binds their other neighbours and allies—including, as yet, Great Britain. It would be foolish, no doubt, to minimize the many strains and stresses to which the young Community is subject, owing partly to disagreement over its long-term objectives and partly to clashes of material interest among its member states. Nevertheless, a glance at the verifiable facts will confirm that the Community is beginning to emerge as an entity in its own right, and that its sense of solidarity is not merely a matter of words.

For eight years now, five basic industrial products—coal, coke, steel, iron ore, and scrap—which account for nearly a quarter of the Community countries' mutual trade, have been free to move throughout the area without paying customs duties or facing quota restrictions. Since January 1, 1959, there have been no such barriers to intra-Community trade in nuclear materials. From the same date, intra-Community tariffs on all other products have been gradually reduced, and now stand at little more

than half their previous level; while quota restrictions on industrial products traded within the Community have almost disappeared. At the same time, the duties levied by the Community
countries on their imports from the rest of the world have begun
to be levelled out into a common external tariff surrounding the
whole area. Currency restrictions between the Community countries have been eased, and timetables have been set for the future
disappearance of those national restrictions which at present prevent or discourage wage-earners and businessmen from working
and settling wherever they choose within the Community. This
is not the whole story; but it suffices to show that the gradual
removal of frontier barriers has begun in earnest.

Meanwhile, industry and business have been making remarkable progress. One of the most striking features of the Community
countries since the war, indeed, has been the amazingly rapid
increase of their gross national product—about 70 per cent in the
ten-year period from 1950 to 1960. Percentages, of course, can be
misleading: the immense percentage growth rates in some
European countries immediately after the war were partly a
reflection of the low level from which their economic recovery
began. But from 1950 onwards, in less abnormal conditions, the
growth rate of the Community countries has been remarkably
steady; and from 1958 to 1961 their gross national product still
showed an overall increase of 21 per cent, while their industrial
production rose by 32 per cent.

Despite what is sometimes suggested, however, these impressive
figures in themselves are no real evidence of the success of European integration: all they show is that it has not thrown the
Community countries into economic disarray. For an index of the
Community's growing cohesion, in fact, one must look at its
internal trade.

Here too the records show immensely rapid growth. Since the
E.C.S.C. was established in 1952, trade in steel within the Community has quadrupled. Since 1958, when the Common Market

Treaty came into force, total trade within the Community has risen by just over 73 per cent—twice as fast as its trade with other countries. From 1960 to 1961 alone, the increase in intra-Community trade was of the order of 16 per cent.

These statistics are undoubtedly significant; but once again the argument *post hoc, ergo propter hoc* is clearly deceptive. Contrary to widely held belief, the figures by no means conclusively prove that the increase of trade within the Community is due to its tariff-cutting process. Intra-Community trade was already expanding rapidly before the Common Market Treaty came into force : from 1955 to 1958, in fact, it increased by 80 per cent. It has even been plausibly argued, therefore, that boom conditions and increasing trade have themselves made tariff-cutting easier, rather than *vice versa*—although this is perhaps merely another version of *post hoc, ergo propter hoc*.[1]

Nevertheless, while it cannot be concluded that the Community's tariff-cutting measures caused the increase in its internal trade, this need not invalidate a more general conclusion. What is significant, indeed, is that throughout this period the economies of the Community countries have been growing more interdependent, creating an economic and commercial solidarity that is helping to reinforce their political cohesion. Moreover, a purely statistical approach to the subject, however sophisticated, risks omitting an extremely important psychological fact.

Ever since 1955, when the Common Market was first publicly mooted, alert businessmen in the Community have been aware that the E.C.S.C.'s tariff-cutting efforts in the field of coal and steel might eventually be supplemented by similar measures covering the whole range of the Community's economy. In company reports and public speeches, as well as in private conversations, one found references to this possibility becoming more and more frequent as the future shape of the Common Market began to emerge. While some greeted the prospect nervously, others saw it as a golden opportunity : and both were anxious to make their plans in advance. By the time the Common Market Treaty came into force in 1958, and even more so by the time its first tariff cuts were made a year later, new investment projects, mergers and agreements, new sales networks and advertising programmes, were already in many cases well beyond the discussion stage. It would be tedious and indeed impossible to list here even such of the new arrangements as have come to light; but examples in the automobile industry alone include a variety of agreements between Renault and Alfa Romeo, between Peugeot and Mercedes-Benz, and between Innocenti and Hans Glas. The Dutch produced their first passenger car shortly after the Common Market Treaty came into force, while Fiat, not to be outdone by their smaller Italians rivals, now have assembly plants in both Belgium and Germany.[2]

More striking to the casual observer, however, is the number of new name-plates on office buildings, most of them in Brussels and Paris, announcing the formation of business and other groups explicitly related to the European Community. On the side of industry, the foremost is the body that now groups the industrial federations of all the Community countries – U.N.I.C.E., *L'Union des industries de la Communauté européenne*. On the labour side, both the Catholic (C.I.S.C.) and the Free (C.I.S.L.) Trade Unions of the Community countries have set up central bureaux to co-ordinate their action. In specific branches of industry and commerce, moreover, there are now about two hundred associations specially established on a Community basis, including ninety concerned with agriculture. In addition to various heavy industries, they quite literally comprise the butcher, the baker, and the candlestick-maker : there is the *Comité des organisations de la boucherie-charcuterie de la Communauté économique européenne* and the *Association des fédérations nationales de la boulangerie et de la boulangerie-patisserie de la C.E.E.*, as well as the *Comité permanent des industries du verre de la C.E.E.* and the *Groupe de travail C.E.E. de la fédération européenne des*

industries de porcelaine et de faience de table et d'ornementation.
New abbreviations include Eurémail (for makers of enamel-
ware), EUROMAISIERS (for maize producers), EUROMALT
(for the malt industry), C.L.I.T.R.A.V.I. (for meat processers),
COLIPED (for bicycle manufacturers), U.N.I.P.E.D.E. (for
electricity producers), GOMAC (for opticians), and G.I.R.P. (for
retail chemists). The Community even has an Association of
Instant Coffee Manufacturers, a Committee of the International
Soap and Detergent Association, and a Union of the Associations
of Fizzy Drinks.

Nor, indeed, are such private ventures confined to the formation of trade associations and business pressure groups. As early
as 1958, a shop-window display in Brussels advertised "The
Refrigerator of the Common Market". "Eurocalza", a new
Italian brand of stockings now on sale throughout the Community in quadrilingual packaging (English, French, German,
and Italian), claims to be "the stocking for the woman of the
new Europe". More recently still, a "European raincoat" has
been launched, complete with price tickets carrying the letters
EUR and six stars, one for each Community country. Department stores, in collaboration with Community wholesalers, have
several times run "Common Market Fortnights", during which
goods from other Community countries are sold at reduced prices
to anticipate the effect of future tariff cuts. In a Brussels store,
one of the most successful of such recent stunts was a display of
Community foodstuffs under the appetizing title of "Europe on
Your Plate".

It would be easy, of course, to overstress the significance of
such salesmen's enterprises; but they may none the less be straws
in the wind—practical evidence, at the consumer's level, of growing economic integration. Furthermore, just as industrialists,
businessmen and trade-union officials in the Community countries
are getting to know one another better, so in Government and
civil service circles there is increasing contact between the national

administrations. In some degree, this is a normal feature of the modern world, evident no less in the expert committees of the United Nations or of the General Agreement on Tariffs and Trade than in specifically European organisations : but here once again the process is carried very much further in the institutions of the European Community.

These institutions are at present a rather curious amalgam, not only because they combine and partially fuse three Community organizations established at different times—the E.C.S.C., the Common Market, and Euratom—but also because their structure itself is a blend of both novel, federal elements and more classical, international features such as are found in bodies like the Council of Europe and the O.E.E.C. There will be more to say of this hybrid aspect later. Here, however, it may be more to the point to emphasize some of those novel elements that are themselves a part of the new pattern which this chapter seeks to describe.

The essential, decision-making institution of the European Community is the Council of Ministers—more properly, the Councils of Ministers, since legally speaking each of the three Community organizations has its own separate Council, although in practice the same Ministers often sit in each, only their advisers changing places as one topic succeeds another. The Council resembles that of any traditional international organization in that its members are national representatives : but it differs from traditional practice in several important respects. In the first place, its powers under the European Community Treaties are more direct, since in many cases its decisions are immediately binding upon the citizens of member states. Secondly, certain of those decisions—and more of them as time goes on—may be taken by majority vote, thereby avoiding obstruction from a national veto. Thirdly, the Council can in most instances only reach a decision if specific proposals have been made, and a draft decision prepared, by an independent "European Executive"— one for each Community organization—whose members, unlike the Ministers, do not represent their national states. Finally, perhaps more intangibly, anyone who has listened to the Council's deliberations cannot fail to be struck by their informal, sometimes almost boardroom atmosphere—again markedly different from that of most international conclaves.

A similar, if less pronounced, sense of intimacy also distinguishes the sessions of the European Parliament, the advisory Assembly of the European Community, common to the E.C.S.C., the Common Market, and Euratom. At present composed of 142 delegates nominated by the national Parliaments from among their own members, this normally meets in the cream-and-brown debating chamber of the Council of Europe building in Strasbourg; but its members, unlike those of the Council of Europe's Consultative Assembly, sit not in alphabetical order round the hemicycle, but in "supranational" political groups. For the most part, except over issues where the purely national interest of all political parties coincides, they speak and act as Community Socialists, Community Liberals, or Community Christian Democrats, as the case may be. Furthermore, although the Assembly has not yet acquired the legislative powers of a true Parliament, it already enjoys important rights, including that of forcing the resignation of any of the European "Executives" by a two-thirds majority vote of no confidence. So far, like Robinson Crusoe's boat, such a vote has proved too weighty to move; but the European Parliament has also to be consulted on a number of Community matters before the Council of Ministers can legally take decisions upon them; and at all stages of their preparation, in addition to putting Parliamentary questions to which an answer is obligatory, it makes its views known and its influence felt through thirteen Standing Committees which hold frequent and often outspoken private "hearings" with members of the European "Executives".

"Informal" is the last word that would be appropriate to describe the third Institution of the European Community, its

Court of Justice. This, like the European Parliament, is also common to the E.C.S.C., the Common Market, and Euratom. Its seven judges, chosen for their undisputed eminence and completely above suspicion of national bias, act chiefly as a supreme court of appeal against failures to respect the Community Treaties and against decisions or rulings of the Community Institutions, as well as in cases of inter-state disputes on Community affairs. The most august of the Community's Institutions, it maintains an outward solemnity appropriate to its rôle as a supranational arbiter whose judgments are final for both individuals and Governments. Its senior officials, like its Judges, are scrupulous in preserving a slightly aloof detachment within the stately white walls of the Villa Vauban in Luxembourg; and it is quite in keeping with the Court's unassailable prestige that the members of the European "Executives" should have established the tradition of taking the oath before it, with some ceremony, on their assumption of office.

But if the Court of Justice most clearly incarnates the "supranational" character of the Community, it is the European "Executives" themselves with which visitors to their headquarters in Brussels and Luxembourg are probably most familiar. Certainly, their rôle in the Community's institutions is the most crucial and paradoxical. Its ambiguity is partly expressed by the very word "executive" : for while it is true that in many instances their function is that of an executant, putting into practice the provisions of the Community Treaties or the decisions reached through the complex of the Community's institutions, their members are by no means "executives" in the same sense as members of the British Cabinet or the President of the United States. Their essential characteristic is the independence to which they are pledged by office, as well as by oath. Although they may previously have been Ministers in national Governments, once appointed they are forbidden to solicit or accept instructions from Governments, groups, or individuals. Significantly enough, the only place in the three Community Treaties in which the word "supranational" is mentioned is in the Article of the E.C.S.C. Treaty which calls upon the members of its Executive, the High Authority, to "abstain from all conduct incompatible with the supranational character of their functions".

The powers of the High Authority, as its name implies, are in some respects greater than those of the Common Market or Euratom Executives: it can in fact take many decisions on its own without passing through the Council of Ministers, and it raises its own revenue by levying a tax on coal and steel firms instead of depending on a budget financed and approved by member Governments. While this reflects a general political climate more federal-minded in 1951, when the E.C.S.C. Treaty was signed, than when the Common Market and Euratom Treaties were concluded six years later, it also follows naturally from the more limited scope of the High Authority's powers. In the narrower field of coal and steel, that is, the Governments themselves were able to lay down more detailed Treaty rules that could be devised in advance for all the remainder of the Community's economy. Euratom, concerned with atomic power and research, is an intermediate case: for if, on general political grounds, the powers of its executive Commission are more limited than those of the E.C.S.C.'s High Authority, they are also technically greater than those of the Common Market's executive Commission because they apply to a more restricted field. There is no doubt, however, that the Common Market Commission wields far more influence than its specific powers on paper would suggest. This was most strikingly evident at the outset of negotiations for British membership of the Community, in November 1961, when the member Government's initial statements were all indirectly based on drafts prepared by the Commission. In some cases, moreover, even the specific powers of the Commission have been increased since the Treaty came into force: it is now empowered—to take but one example—to fine transport firms which practise discrimination and any firms which form cartels. Its normal rôle, however, has been well defined as threefold : it acts as an independent stimulus to Community action, as an impartial watchdog to ensure respect of the Treaty (on which it has already taken several member Governments to Court), and as a kind of "honest broker" to help bring about agreement among the Community's member states. If this complex of functions falls far short of those of a federal executive, it clearly surpasses the normal attributes of a mere secretariat, and covers legal and political territory whose novelty is attested by the number of words in inverted commas which its description has involved.

The Community's many visitors, whether to the old brownstone building of the High Authority in Luxembourg—formerly the headquarters of the Grand Duchy's state railways—or to the impersonal white office blocks of the Common Market and Euratom Commissions in Brussels, have often in fact reported on the novelty of its atmosphere. In Brussels, they may have been struck by the sight of red, white and blue "European" number-plates on the cars of Community officials; in Luxembourg, by the E (for Europe).-shaped building which houses the first of the European Schools, where the children of those officials—and others—are taught in four languages on a special syllabus whose history and geography, in particular, have been lifted out of the national mould into a wider European pattern. In either capital, the newcomer may encounter the familiar features of any international organization—the polyglot secretaries, the busy team of translators, the multi-channel headphones and the interpreters in their glass-fronted cabins. But among the duplicated documents and green steel furniture that are a feature of all the Community offices, it is the European officials themselves—the "Eurocrats", as they have been nicknamed—who leave the most lasting impression.

In all, the "Eurocrats" number well over 3,000—about 1,000 in the High Authority, about 500 in Euratom, and more than

1,900 in the Common Market. "Parkinson's Law" has been cited to explain these figures; but in view of the Community's wide responsibilities, covering trade, finance, labour, transport, and agriculture, as well as other aspects of six countries' economic affairs, the total is comparatively modest—less than half the size, indeed, of the British Board of Trade. Moreover, although like all institutions the Community Executives no doubt harbour a certain proportion of dead wood, outside observers have confirmed my own inevitably partisan impression that at least two qualities distinguish their staff from that of some other international organizations. The first is their generally high calibre. *The Economist*[3] has praised the "dynamism" of these "multilingual tough-minded Europeans mostly aged around 35–40", whom it has described as "Europe's Sanguine Young Men". Most of them are old enough to have had bitter experience of warfare—in World War II, in Indo-China, or elsewhere. They are young enough, on the other hand, to have escaped thorough conditioning by national civil service routine : many of them, in fact, come from industry, business, banking, engineering, or academic life. Themselves the products of a technological civilization, they take for granted its benefits in the form of cars, cine-cameras, or tape-recorders; but enough of them are individualists to avoid the taint of the organization man. If they have a collective fault, it is probably a temptation to intellectual arrogance : but this is offset by the complex, humbling interplay of six separate national traditions and habits of thought. The second notable feature of their organization, indeed, is its successful creation of a joint and purposeful "European" ethos—a Community team spirit that unites the most diverse personalities and talents. In all three Community Executives, the different nationalities are deliberately scrambled, from Directors-General to doormen; and to quote *The Economist* once more, "very often one can't tell what country they come from until one hears their accents . . . the game of guessing national stereotypes is over". Frenchmen, in this crew-cut technocratic context, have lost whatever resemblance they ever had to *la famille Fenouillard*; Italians no longer suggest Private Angelo or even Vittorio De Sica; and young Germans have nothing at all in common with the prewar cartoons of Charles Reynolds in *Punch*.

Although the makers of the European Community have always denied that their aim is to produce European uniformity, this same disappearance of national stereotypes has its fainter counterpart on a wider scale. What is happening in the case of the "Eurocrats" may be a minor portent of the pattern which a visit to any European beach in August will quickly show to be emerging in the Community as a whole. *Time* magazine, in its own happily inimitable manner, has reported it thus : "Meanwhile, back from a summer of skimming with passportless ease all over the Common Market countries were bikini-bronzed girls and tousle-haired boys, members of the new, low-budget international set that motor-scoots and camps with blithe disregard of frontiers —which are often posted with neat new signs proclaiming, 'Another Border But Still Europe'."[4]

It would be naïve to imagine, no doubt, that this foreshadowed the growth of a European patriotism and the withering away of the nation state; but the sense of belonging to a single entity is undoubtedly real among the "Eurocrats", and even among their colleagues in the national civil services. Partly, it arises from the fact of their meeting in innumerable—some would say interminable—expert committees, whose members gradually come to form a kind of European "grapevine", along which gossip and information and influence flow more and more. But it is certainly strongest whenever the representatives of the Community countries find themselves facing the rest of the world.

By the end of the 1960's, if not sooner, the Common Market Treaty prescribes that the Community shall have a joint policy for external trade. Bilateral trade agreements will then be replaced by agreements made by the Community as a whole : trade measures now applied by one or more of the Community's member states—to face Soviet dumping, for instance, or to aid developing countries—will be applied, or not applied, by all. The transition to this collective action will of course be painful, and it threatens to be slow. But already, in modest enough ways, that transition is beginning. Already, the Community has begun to apply a part of its common external tariff; already, it has begun to negotiate as a unit within the G.A.T.T. Already, its member states have agreed to consult each other before concluding any new trade agreements with other countries, and to limit the duration of such new agreements to the time that still has to run before a joint trade policy becomes obligatory under the Common Market Treaty.

All these facts are well-known: but what is less widely realized, outside the Community, is the degree of informal consultation that already takes place. Non-member Governments have sometimes been surprised, I think, to find that hints dropped in one capital—in Rome, say, or in The Hague—quickly become the subject of joint Community discussion, often in Brussels: as a colleague remarked to me recently, *"toutes ces choses se savent à la fin"*. The representatives of member Governments try to coordinate their action, indeed, not only in the Organization for Economic Co-operation and Development—O.E.C.D., the successor to O.E.E.C.—and similar economic bodies, but also in some of the Committees of the United Nations. On several occasions, the Community countries have exhibited jointly in trade fairs and festivals: but what is less generally realized is that outside such high days and holidays the officials of their embassies in non-member countries hold informal but regular meetings and even draw up joint reports. The results of such extra-curricular co-operation are seldom spectacular; but the precedent it sets is highly significant. Taken together with the plans proposed as a result of the Bonn Declaration in July, 1961, it amounts to an extension into the international scene of the solidarity which the Community is beginning to achieve within its own borders. In other words, the Community is not merely an innovation on the map of Europe: it is also a dramatic new feature on the map of the world.

Just how dramatic the change is can be seen in a few statistics. Taken singly, none of the Community's member states has a population of more than about 50 million—roughly that of the British Isles. Together, they have a combined population of 170 million—nearly as many as the United States. Their active population, indeed, is even greater than that of the United States —73 million as compared with 69 million. Taken as a whole, the Community is the world's second largest steel producer, and in 1960—when the recession hit American steel production—it was the first. Above all, it is the world's biggest trading power, its biggest importer, its second biggest exporter, and its biggest buyer of raw materials. Its emergence as a new unit on the world scene, therefore, is comparable to that of the United States in the nineteenth century and of the U.S.S.R. in the twentieth. It is a new giant in a world where only giants rule.

The Italians, always linguistically inventive, have coined the word *ridimensionamento* to describe the fundamental change of scale to which André Malraux once referred when he pointed out that continents had replaced countries as the effective units of world power. It is a word that sums up also the dilemma with which the Community's emergence faced the United Kingdom, itself still powerful, and in absolute terms perhaps more powerful than before, but nevertheless relatively less so when compared with the giant on its doorstep. Nor was Great Britain alone in her embarrassment: for the United States will also face the problem of *ridimensionamento* if the Community's economic power goes on growing, and especially with the addition of Great Britain and other countries. Fortunately, the history of European integration shows that such problems can also be opportunities.

CHAPTER II

THE POLITICAL BACKGROUND

Europe, like Italy in Metternich's phrase, is *"ein geographischer Begriff"*, a geographical expression; but it is also an idea, a slogan, a rallying-cry, and a cliché. Although its meanings have varied throughout the centuries, some of them still awaken echoes for continental Europeans. It is worthwhile, therefore, to glance at the word's changing overtones, if only to see which of them survive among its connotations today.

The word *Europe* itself first appears as the subject of a Greek myth—the story of Europa, daughter of the King of Tyre in what is now the Lebanon, carried off to Crete by Zeus in the guise of a bull. It used to be thought that this legend symbolized the Hellenization of the Semitic word for "West", *erib*— a root surviving in the Arabic word *Maghreb*, and perhaps most vividly translated by the German *Abendland*. Now, however, scholars tend to derive the word from Greek roots : some, referring to the adjective εὐρωπός, suggest that it means "broad", while others, conjoining εὐρύς (broad) and ὄψις or ὀπτίλος, with optical connotations, have variously interpreted it as "broad-faced" or "far-seeing". Its first geographical application, in the post-Homeric *Hymn to Apollo*, was to the Greek mainland as distinct from the Aegean islands; but it soon acquired a wider meaning. Herodotus was puzzled by its etymology : all he knew was that it distinguished Europe—illogically, he thought—from Africa and Asia.

This notion of *contrast* reappears, with much force, later in Europe's history; but in the Graeco-Roman era the name

29

"Europe" itself was comparatively little used. The Mediterranean, indeed, was the centre of classical civilization rather than its southern or eastern limit : the Roman Empire in particular embraced much of North Africa and the Near East. This is not to say, of course, that Greece and Rome were not decisive in determining much of the content of what is usually regarded as the European tradition. Even now, rather as a piece of pumice stone in a modern bathroom may serve as a *memento mori* recalling the inferno that rages beneath the earth's crust, so such words as "electromatic" and "television" recall the classical origins of even the least Augustan specimens of twentieth-century terminology. Better words like "democracy" and "justice" are a reminder that the classical influence is not merely linguistic. Roman law, indeed, is probably the most significant and lasting mark that Rome left on Europe. Implicit in it were not only the ideals of Roman conduct—*pietas, humanitas, libertas, auctoritas, fides, disciplina, gravitas, constantia*—but also the notion of a *universal community*, transcending tribal, national, or racial barriers. At the same time, however, the notion of contrast persisted in the distinction between *Latinitas* and *barbaria*—although this was not yet geographically identified with the distinction between Europe and the rest of the world.

The paradox became clearer with the emergence of Christianity as the religion of the Empire and the subsequent growth of the medieval Church. While on the one hand the Church's claims and ideals were universal, on the other there gradually arose the concept of "Christendom" (*christianitas*) as a geographical unit embracing "the faithful", adherents of *christianismus*; and both Latin terms were sometimes confused. Moreover, as the Moslem invaders pressed further westwards and northwards, Christendom became more and more identified, *de facto*, with Europe. It is perhaps significant that the word "Europeans" (*Europeenses*) is first used by an eighth-century chronicler in a description of the battle of Tours in 732, at which the Moslems were defeated by

Charles Martel. The neologism was necessary because Charles's forces included both Roman Gauls and "barbarians"; but if this implied a distinction between Christendom and Europe, it was clear that the notion of a European entity was gaining ground. In the following century, Charlemagne was described as *"rex pater Europae"* and *"apex Europae"*, the father of Europe and the head of Europe. The notion of contrast had now become even more specific; for in these rather flowery tributes Charlemagne's Empire was now being distinguished not only from Africa and Asia and from the world of the Moslems, but also from that of the Emperor in Constantinople and the Greek part of the Church. As one historian has put it, *"Europa* and *ecclesia* are, within this conceptual framework, identical : they constitute the political expression of the union of all Latin Christians, that is, the union of all 'Romani'."[1]

In some respects this concept hardened with successive clashes between Rome and Constantinople; but seldom after Charlemagne were the idea of Europe and that of Latin Christendom so closely identified again until the later middle ages. This was partly due to the restatement of universalist claims by the eleventh-century reformers of the Roman Church. In the so-called East-West "schism" of 1054, the reforming Cardinal Humbert treated the Patriarch of Constantinople merely as an erring Bishop; and Pope Gregory VII a few years later pointedly stated that "the law of the Popes embraces more territory than does imperial law". In 1095, launching the first Crusade at the Council of Clermont, Pope Urban II is credited with the explicit distinction between Christendom and Europe : he was reported as saying,

There remains Europe, the third continent. How small is the part of it inhabited by us Christians! For none would term Christian those barbarous people who live in distant islands on the frozen ocean, for they live in the manner of brutes. And even this fragment of our world is attacked by the Turks and Saracens.[2]

Earlier, moreover, the same account quotes Urban as affirming that Christians should "share the inhabited earth equally with the enemies of God"—words which suggest that, in the chronicler's mind at least, Europe was only accidentally the heartland of Christendom.

Nevertheless, the medieval Church left its mark on the secular concept of Europe. As the Papacy reached it apogee and declined in the later middle ages, first its own organization and achievements, and then the various reactions against them, were on a European scale. Meanwhile, the Crusades had helped to emphasize the contrast between Europe and the Near-Eastern outposts of *"l'oultremer"*. The combined result was that even when imperial and ecclesiastical bonds were slackened and broken, a secular notion of "Europe" succeeded them, and one which carried with it some of the reflected glory—and latent self-satisfaction—inherent in the idea of "Christendom".

The use of the word "Europe", in fact, became more frequent and more telling in the fourteenth and fifteenth centuries. On at least one of the occasions when Dante employed it, for example, the context evoked some of the superior overtones of "Christendom": refuting the idea that the Church conferred temporal power on the Emperor, he added: "not only do Asians and Africans reject this notion, but even most natives of Europe do so too." Other similarly significant uses of the word can be found in writers as far apart as Matthew Paris and Petrarch.[3]

Even the Papal schism of the late fourteenth and early thirteenth centuries, deeply involved as it was in national rivalries and animosities, still produced in the Conciliar Movement an attempt on the part of Europe's secular rulers to solve what was regarded as a common problem; and although the outcome fell far short of unity or even dignity, what is noteworthy is the distress with which disunity was greeted. A French pamphleteer in 1399 aptly summarized his dismay: "The pagan world can exclaim 'Christendom is finished!' . . . One tongue hates another tongue, each nation its neighbour."[4] It was a cry that was to be echoed down the centuries.

One of the most obvious features, indeed, of the transition from "medieval" to "modern" Europe was the growth of the nation state. At the same time, however, by a curious paradox, three of the features usually associated with that transition also helped to reinforce the secular concept of Europe.

The first was the fall of Constantinople to the Turks in 1453. This ominously dramatized and brought closer to Europe the struggle of which successive Crusades had been a more distant symbol; and it also gave a different emphasis to the notion of Crusading. When Pius II, the great Renaissance Pope, proposed a further Eastward expedition, the Congress of Mantua in 1459 gave a new twist to his proposal. This time, according to the Mantua resolution, the aim of the Crusade was no longer to liberate Jerusalem, but "to drive the Turk out of Europe".[5]

Meanwhile, the "humanism" of the Renaissance itself was giving further currency to the idea of *"Europa"*. *"Christianitas"*, formerly almost its synonym, was objectionable to Renaissance men of letters on two grounds: first, because it could not be fitted into hexameters, and secondly, more generally, because it was not classical Latin. The latter objection applied also to the word *"Christianus"*, for which Pius II in particular substituted *"Europaeus"* in innumerable passages of his writings. Pictorially, likewise the Renaissance brought Europe to the fore, as its artists now began to personify not only the Europa of Greek legend but also the "Europa" of an increasing number of maps.

These, in turn, were the sign as well as the instrument of a third new influence that encouraged what might now be called a growing European consciousness: that is, the voyages and discoveries of the Renaissance—which used to figure, indeed, in the

Cambridge history syllabus as part of "The Expansion of Europe". Not only did the new maps help to make ideas of geography more precise and accurate : they also made clearer the contrasts between Europe and other continents, beside which the differences between European countries looked comparatively small. Some of the maps, in particular, indicated which territories were Christian and which were not—indispensable data for all but the rashest or best-armed traveller, and a further confirmation of Europe's identity. One of them even embodied that identity in a strange blend of cartoon and cartography showing Europe as a queen, viewed from Eastwards, with the Iberian Peninsula as her head, Italy as her right arm, and Denmark as her left; the British Isles were shown floating over her shoulder like a streamer from the sceptre in her left hand. This was in 1588;[6] but as early as 1530 a geographer could speak quite naturally as *"nostra Europa"*, *"our Europe"*. The note of pride was echoed in the next century by the travel-writer (and armchair traveller) Samuel Purchas : "The Qualitie of Europe," he declared, "exceeds her Quantitie, in this the least, in that the best of the World"—and plunged into an excited account of Europe's colonial conquests and her "civilizing mission" as the bearer not only of faith, but of technology, science, cookery, and horse-management.[7] In Purchas, indeed, Christendom's sense of superiority had been secularized with a vengeance; and by the eighteenth century, Europeans had become quite accustomed to seeing the world as Europe's oyster. When Cabot had set sail at the end of the fifteenth century, his commission from the King had urged him to explore for lands "unknown to all Christians" : but when Commodore John Byron put to sea over 250 years later, his orders were to seek "land and islands of great extent hitherto unvisited by any European power".[8] Europe's self-consciousness had entered the language of modern diplomacy.

Diplomacy, in the sense of organized relations between sovereign states, is indeed a characteristic feature of post-

Renaissance Europe; and in itself it embodies two out of the three main themes that next pervade the story. The first is that of national—and colonial—rivalry between the European powers: France, Spain, the House of Hapsburg, England, Prussia, and Russia, dominated first by the Hapsburgs and later by the Bourbons. The second is a general European recognition of the need for some check upon both rivalry and dominance— a check at first empirical, then more consciously formulated as "the balance of power", "the concert of Europe", or "the system of alliances". In various forms, this system of check and balance among the powers survived in European diplomacy until 1917, when the military deadlock between two equal and opposing groups of armies in the trenches was only broken after the intervention of the United States. The Versailles peace conference deliberately sought to put an end to the balance-of-power system in Europe; but it had little to put in its place beyond the principle of "self-determination" which brought back national rivalries and national dominance in another guise.

These twin themes, of rivalry and dominance on the one hand, and on the other repeated attempts at international order and balance, make a familiar, unedifying, and in some ways unilluminating story. A third theme, however, is worth developing in more detail. This is the theme of a continual hankering after some kind of European unity. It was a theme that recurred chiefly in the writings of intellectuals: until the present century it was only spasmodically taken up by statesmen, and then usually distorted, sometimes monstrously. Nor, quite naturally, did it take anything like the same form at different times. Nevertheless, it too left its trace on present-day ideas of "Europe"; and its varying modulations moreover echoed some of the social and political changes that were to transform modern Europe out of recognition. Obviously enough, its various motifs were frequently confused and intertwined, but for the sake of clarity they may be considered one by one.

One of the earliest, perhaps, was an often mistaken nostalgia for the ideal of a united Christendom—a nostalgia already apparent in the writings of Conciliar pamphleteers. In the political sphere, Conciliar theory lay behind the famous projects of Pierre Dubois at the beginning of the fourteenth century. These proposed a European confederation, to be ruled by a European Council of "wise, expert, and faithful men", representing "the Most Christian Republic", but with the right of appeal to the Holy See. Although in fact neither Papal nor Imperial, this plan had a typically medieval aim and title—"*De recuperatione Terre Sancte*", "About the Recovery of the Holy Land". A similar pretext for unity was adduced by Antoine Marigny, the French adventurer who in 1464 proposed to the King of Bohemia "to emancipate peoples and kings by the organization of a new Europe"; and although the subsequent efforts of Bohemia, Poland, and Hungary were again directed against both the Pope and the Emperor, they nevertheless sought to establish "a Diet and Assembly of Christian Kings and Princes".[9]

The Reformation, while it altered the lineaments of "Christendom", by no means destroyed it as a concept. Luther and Calvin both sought to protect Christian unity by means of a general council; and in England Richard Hooker, the most sophisticated theorist of the Elizabethan church settlement, thought in terms of what has been well described as "a decentralized Christendom . . . whose unity was effected by the voluntary consent of the member Churches"[10]—a kind of ecclesiastical *Europe des Patries*.

The motif of nostalgia indeed lingered, reaching its best-known expression in the "Grand Design" of the Protestant Duc de Sully, once attributed to King Henri IV of France. This proposed for Europe a "Most Christian Council", and called upon the Germans to unite "first among themselves" and then "with their ancient, loyal, and courageous friends and allies", since "under Charlemagne the name of the Germans, the Gauls, and the Franks was but as a single nation".[11] A somewhat similar approach was that of the German philosopher Leibniz, who in 1691 wrote hopefully of the day when "union will be achieved, catholicity will be restored, Germany and the Latin world will recover their spiritual communion, the United Provinces and England will in their turn re-enter a Church at once Roman and reformed, and believers, all believers, will oppose the forces of disintegration that threaten their faith".[12]

It was a note that the Romantics were to strike again later, and one that was to echo in the Holy Alliance of 1815. Long before, however, a second and more modern motif had been heard. This was the quest for "perpetual peace"—a natural enough reaction to the use of gunpowder in war.

Already, Pierre Dubois had declared that "to ensure peace, it is not enough to praise its benefits or even to agree to keep it. War must be prevented by suitable institutions". The same motive inspired Emeric Crucé in 1623, when he proposed as "a means of establishing a General Peace" an Assembly at which "all sovereigns would have permanent ambassadors". Grotius in 1625 significantly entitled his monumental appeal to natural law *"De iure belli et pacis"*, "On the Law of War and Peace". Sully's Grand Design, too, proposed peace as one of its objects— to be kept by means of a European army; while peace was likewise the concern of the English Quaker William Penn, founder of Pennsylvania, when in 1693 he published his *Essay towards the Present and Future Peace of Europe*, proposing "a European Diet, Parliament, or State". One of the most elaborate of such projects was that of the Abbé de Saint Pierre, whose *Mémoires pour rendre la paix perpétuelle en Europe* appeared in 1712. This work proposed a perpetual alliance between European sovereigns and the rule of a "European Senate" backed by collective sanctions : the pact was to be subject to revision by majority voting except on fundamental issues, where unanimity was to apply.

"Suitable institutions", "permanent ambassadors", a "European Parliament", a European army, majority voting—all these phrases and ideas, anachronistically, have a practical ring today. The hope of perpetual peace, too, was perennial throughout the years that followed. Jeremy Bentham, for example, devoted a whole chapter to it in his *Principles of International Law*, written in 1789 although unpublished until fifty years later. Immanuel Kant's treatise on *Perpetual Peace*, which appeared in 1795, was only the most famous of a number of similar works. Typical of their aspirations was a book published in 1850 by Victor Considérant, a disciple of the French sociologist, Charles Fourier. This was entitled *La dernière guerre et la paix définitive en Europe*—words that were echoed later in the 1914 slogan "The War to End War". The same frail hope inspired the League of Nations, itself in many ways a body essentially European. "We are here to see," President Woodrow Wilson told the Versailles Peace Conference, "that the very foundations of this war are swept away".[13]

But if the longing for perpetual peace was a constant element in the fitful search for unity among European nations, the eighteenth century had added a further motif. The Abbé de Saint-Pierre, like so many victims of satire, was as famous for his detractors as for his achievements: he was mercilessly lampooned by both Jean-Jacques Rousseau and Voltaire. Yet if both were sceptical of the Abbé's projects, the name of Voltaire at least is a reminder that in the "Age of Reason" Europe achieved a degree of cultural cosmopolitanism that in turn furthered and enriched its hankering after unity.

In some respects, Europe's cosmopolitanism reflected genuine similarities among its nations. Economically, its basic structure at the beginning of the eighteenth century was still largely agricultural. Socially, it still had a population predominantly peasant, with a strong aristocracy and an influential church hierarchy. Politically, it was still under the sway of powerful dynastic monarchies. Against this background, it was natural for "culture" to be international. Even reactions against the old order tended to be homogeneous, under the intellectual leadership of French rationalism as represented by the Encyclopaedists and the *philosophes*. The so-called "enlightened despots" adopted French writers and artists : Voltaire's uneasy sojourn at the court of Frederick the Great was a characteristic episode in the career of so European a figure. In England Edward Gibbon and Jeremy Bentham, in Holland Belle de Zuylen ("Zélide") wrote in French as fluently as in their own languages. The Grand Tour, however uncomfortable and hazardous, took well-to-do young men into a cosmopolitan European society. It was Montesquieu who said that Germany was made for travelling in, Italy for staying in, England for thinking in, and France for living in; it was Voltaire who pointed out that a Frenchman, an Englishman, and a German might be mistaken for inhabitants of the same town. But it was an Irishman, Edmund Burke, who summed up the general feeling most succinctly when he remarked in 1797 that "no citizen of Europe could be altogether an exile in any part of it".[14] Out of such assumptions of cultural unity came few projects for political union : but it was typical of those which did that Kant's proposal for a confederation of free states was based on the conviction that war was condemned by Reason, the guiding light to which all Europe felt that it owed allegiance.

Nor, indeed, did Europe's cultural unity go into eclipse even after the "Age of Reason" and even when culture itself became more deeply rooted in national life. In the world of music, Verdi, Wagner, Dvořák, and Rimsky-Korsakov, each the embodiment of national aspirations, were nevertheless European figures; in literature, likewise, the nineteenth century saw the conclusion of copyright laws and conventions which facilitated and protected cultural interchange. What was true in the artistic sphere extended also into science and economics, so that as one historian has put it, "the nineteenth century enjoyed, under the leadership of Anglo-Saxon banking, German science, and French art and manners, a kind of European and almost worldwide unity".[15]

The last phrase is a reminder that as the eighteenth century drew to an end a further motif, itself partly coloured by the ideals of the "Age of Reason", came from outside Europe to suggest analogies which were thereafter to haunt all future thinking about European unity. This was the American Revolution and the successful establishment of the United States.

George Washington himself, in a letter to Lafayette, was among the first to draw the analogy and to prophesy that there would one day be a "United States of Europe".[16] Kant toyed with the comparison only to reject it; but the French philosopher Saint-Simon in 1814 clearly based his plan for "the reorganization of European society" on a study of the American Constitution. As Francesco Crispi, the Italian Liberal, said later, "the idea of the United States of Europe is in the air". Victor Hugo never tired of proclaiming it; Pierre-Joseph Proudhon preached it; and it even became the title of a periodical. The phrase was used, in varying senses and not always approvingly, by the Paris section of the First International, by Lenin, and by Trotsky; and the same analogy was considered, though not confirmed, by the Congress of Political Sciences which met in Paris in 1900. Its last appearance before World War II was in Count Coudenhove-Kalergi's "Pan-Europe" movement of the 1920's, whose plans for European union bore many resemblances to the political structure of the U.S.A.

While the American Revolution, however, was consolidating itself in the new world, another was taking place in the old. The French Revolution of 1789, with its universalist ideals, was in part a product of the "Age of Reason"; but it quickly turned into something very different. When it culminated in the Napoleonic Empire, a new and strident motif was added to the theme of European unity. At the end of his life, Napoleon recommended to his heirs "to unite Europe in indissoluble federative bonds": but his own attempt to do so had been that of the "armed missionaries" whose unpopularity Robespierre had already predicted. "I wanted to tame Europe by violence," he afterwards admitted: "today it must be convinced by ideas alone."[17] It was a lesson that Adolf Hitler's Third Reich had to be taught all over again.

Napoleon saw himself not only as "a crowned Washington" but also as a medieval Emperor. "I am not the successor of Louis XIV," he declared, "but of Charlemagne." This, clearly, was the nostalgic and visionary language of the Romantic movement, which also in its turn added a motif to the theme of unity. The poet Novalis in Germany and Chateaubriand in France both looked back to a medieval ideal—the former to "Europe or Christendom", the latter to a time when the Papacy had been "on the point of realizing this beautiful dream" of "a tribunal in Europe which would judge nations and monarchs in the name of God".[18] Some such vision of Christendom underlay the Holy Alliance set up by the Tsar in 1815, whereby Austria, Prussia, and Russia herself undertook "to consider themselves all as members of one Christian nation". But although the plan was endorsed by the majority of European sovereigns, at least three leading statesmen remained unconvinced. In England, Lord Castlereagh described it as "a piece of sublime mysticism and nonsense"; Talleyrand called it "a ludicrous contract"; and Metternich dismissed it as "a high-sounding Nothing".[19]

The visionary motif also drew support from the nineteenth century's optimism and faith in "science", concomitant with rapid economic expansion in Europe and overseas. The positivist Auguste Comte, for example, proposed to apply his philosophic system to a so-called "Western republic" almost exactly coinciding, geographically, with the European Community of today; and others beside Victor Hugo dreamed that "in the twentieth century there will be an extraordinary nation . . . illustrious, rich, thoughtful, peaceable, friendly towards the rest of mankind. . . . Sewers will be replaced by drainage, punishment by teaching; prisons will be transformed into schools. . . . This nation will have

Paris as its capital, and will not be called France : it will be called Europe".

It is perhaps characteristic that both the Holy Alliance and Victor Hugo spoke of "a nation" : for nineteenth-century Romantic nationalism, by a curious paradox, also coloured the idea of Europe. If Bismarck's *Blut und Eisen* policy was frankly nationalistic, earlier German federalism was not; and if Cavour was in many respects a traditional diplomat, Giuseppe Mazzini, the founder of "Young Italy" and prophet of Italian unity, also founded "Young Europe" in the hope of achieving what he had earlier called "the moral unity of Europe in a democratic republic which must lead to the federation of peoples". "Young Europe" was set up in 1834. Fourteen years later, in 1848, Europe was swept by the wave of abortive revolutions in which, as the positivist Emile Littré wrote in *Le National*, "the sentiment of European brotherhood grows as the revolution spreads and the democratic cause makes new converts".[20]

This was the most dramatic outward sign of the social and economic forces that were at work like yeast beneath the surface of European politics—population growth, increased urbanization, the spread of industrialism, and the emergence of a politically conscious popular movement. It was with these changes that one further motif was added to the theme of Europe's fumbling quest for unity—the motif of international socialism, of which the prophet, in this context, was Proudhon. His career spanned the first half of the nineteenth century; and in his two last works, *Du principe fédératif* (1863) and *De la capacité politique des classes ouvrières* (1865), he drew together the strands of all his thinking in what has since become something of a *vade-mecum* for many European federalists. Federation or confederation, he thought, was necessary if only to safeguard the interests of smaller countries : he was at once scornful and nervous of more classical alliances in which the weaker partners risked subordination to "a great European monarchy". "The twentieth century," he insisted, "will open the era of federations, or mankind will once more begin a purgatory lasting for a thousand years."[21]

The immediate influence of Proudhon's writings on Europe, however, was not great. A few disciples continued his teachings, chiefly in the Swiss Jura; but despite a revival of interest in him in France just before World War I, the traces of his doctrine petered out among the parochial lucubrations of anarchists, regionalists, and cranks. Meanwhile, international socialism took other paths. Despite Karl Marx's dictum that "the working classes have no country", he himself held that "the chimeras of a European republic, of perpetual peace under a political organization have become as grotesque as talk of the union of peoples under the aegis of universal free trade". Similarly, despite the attempts of the French and German branches of the International to make contact on the eve of the Franco-Prussian War of 1870, Friedrich Engels gently derided "these people who are completely dominated by grandiose phrases", and Marx avowedly hoped for a Prussian victory because "the preponderance of the German proletariat over the French proletariat will mean at the same time the victory of our theory over that of Proudhon".[22] Lenin likewise gave plans for European unity second or third place : "in a capitalist régime," he wrote, "the United States of Europe will be either impossible or reactionary." Of all the Communist leaders, in fact, only Leon Trotsky was less categorical, suggesting with what looks like remarkable foresight that "not only the question of the Ruhr, that is of European fuel and metal, but also the question of repartition, may perfectly well be settled in the framework of a United States of Europe".[23]

What was true of the Communists in this respect was for a long time true of the Socialists. Despite the efforts of the Second International, Socialism in Europe divided into national movements : as the Italian Socialist author Ignazio Silone himself put it, of all the nationalizations advanced by Socialism, that which succeeded best was the nationalization of Socialism itself. Nevertheless, international and European aims still lingered, particularly in the trade union movement. In 1889, European leather workers set up an international federation, followed by similar organizations for miners and metal, textile, and transport workers. At the turn of the century, the national trade-union federations of Great Britain, Germany, and Scandinavia began the process of consultation and affiliation that by 1913 culminated in the establishment of the International Federation of Trade Unions, representing the majority of organized labour in most European countries. When after World War I Socialist or Social-Democratic Governments were returned in a number of European countries, Socialists in particular began once more to feel an international tug on their patriotic loyalties. This same kind of divided allegiance, of course, was felt still more strongly by European Communists; but even people without political affiliations were made aware of wider horizons in ways that later prepared them to accept the idea of European unity. In 1927, an American traveller with no particular axe to grind reported : "Many of the common people I talked with in Europe see no salvation for the suspicious squabbling continent but a United States of Europe—if only the antiquated statesmen would realize it."[24]

World War I, as it happened, helped to awaken just such a realization. It is difficult at this distance to recall the shock with which 1914 was greeted—especially in England : not for nothing did a whole generation call the conflict "The Great War" or simply "The War". The appalling losses of citizens' armies were only part of the reason : there was also the feeling that a kind of community in Europe had been destroyed. One can sense this, for instance, in the twenty years' correspondence between André Gide and Rainer Maria Rilke. Before the war, the French novelist and the German poet exchanged letters in leisurely French like two survivors from the eighteenth century : afterwards, following a six-year silence, Rilke wrote of "the moment of disaster", "the crumbling of a world", and both complained of the complications of passports and frontier formalities, looking back with aged nostalgia to "the journeys of long ago".[25]

It was only after World War I, in fact, that statesmen began seriously to study the possibility of unity in Europe—first in the League of Nations, and later, more specifically, in the proposals of Aristide Briand. Briand had been honorary President of Coudenhove-Kalergi's Pan-European Union, and when he became Prime Minister of France he was the first—and so far as I know the only—holder of that office to announce as part of his programme the founding of "the United States of Europe". The so-called "Briand Memorandum" which followed in 1930 was somewhat vague, as were the friendly but non-committal replies of the governments to which it was sent. Later that year it was buried in a special Study Committee of the League of Nations; and all that came of the project was a series of meetings which ended with Briand's death in 1932. Already, indeed, events in Europe had been moving faster than men's reactions to them. In the very year of the Briand proposals, the German Nazi party won its first great victory in the *Reichstag*, and the political pre-history of unity in Europe rapidly drew to an end. It took twenty more years, and another World War, for the real work to begin.

From this survey of the evolving idea of Europe a number of themes has already emerged: the influence of the classical world, and especially of Roman Law; the imprint of Christianity; the unity achieved by the medieval Empire and the Papacy; the sense of solidarity embodied in the notion of Crusading; post-medieval nostalgia for a past often misunderstood; the longing for perpetual peace; the effects of cosmopolitan culture; the example of the United States; the imperialism of Napoleon; Romanticism and nationalism; international Socialism, federalism, and the growth of a European Trade Union movement. All these in their time contributed to the notion of Europe, and some of them are still influential in the Europe of today.

Continental Europeans, in particular, have a strong sense of history; and many supporters of European integration, as well as its opponents, have drawn modern comparisons with various stages of its past. Obviously, all of them cannot be entirely right: nor, I think, are all of them completely mistaken. The "European" movement of the present day bears the traces of its history; but it is also something more than the sum of its tributaries.

Roman Law, for instance, left with the peoples it touched most deeply both a preference for starting from stated principles and a bent for codified legislation that contrasts with the more empirical procedures of Anglo-Saxon case-law: in the present-day European Community, its strict ghost can perhaps be detected haunting the Treaty of Rome. On the other hand, however, the working of Community law relies heavily on accumulated jurisprudence, and the interpretation of the Community Treaties has always shown great respect for stubborn and irreducible fact.

Similarly, while it is true that for obvious reasons many Catholics are among the most vocal supporters of European integration, only a minority among them can fairly be described as "medieval", and serious Catholic historians have shared with their Protestant colleagues the task of severely qualifying the popular image of the Middle Ages as a more or less static continuum of Imperial unity and Papal faith. Moreover, although some of the key statesmen of postwar Europe—Schuman, De Gasperi, Adenauer, de Gaulle—have been Catholics, sometimes visited by nostalgic visions, others are of a very different stamp. A distinguished Englishman once described Jean Monnet to me as "a buccaneer"—words which I took to be a compliment: but he could hardly have been called "Carolingian", despite his holding the 1953 "Charlemagne Prize" awarded by the City of Aachen, centre of Charlemagne's court, to modern statesmen who have contributed to European unity. Again, of the nine present members of the Common Market Commission, two are

reputedly Socialists and at least two more—including its President, Professor Walter Hallstein—are Protestants. Finally,
although all the Community countries have Catholic political
parties, their support alone would never have sufficed to carry the
movement forward had it not been much more broadly based.

The analogy with the Crusades looks at first sight a little more
promising. Extremist militants have sometimes used language
which suggests that they see "Christendom" as once more
threatened by infidels from the East; and in a totally different
context the word *"oultremer"* from the Crusading epoch reappears in the phrase *"pays et territoires d'outre-mer"*, used to
describe former dependencies, chiefly in Africa, where some
Europeans have professed a "civilizing mission". In a more
general sense, the "European" movement has undoubtedly pro-
fited from a kind of pioneering enthusiasm, backed by the
dangerous sense of belonging to an élite. For some of the young
and once-young men at work in Luxembourg and Brussels during the past ten years, it is this which redeems demanding,
humdrum, and sometimes exasperating tasks, performed under
pressure through long hours in rooms filled with cigarette-smoke
and multilingual argument. But if this is "crusading", it is also
practical and hard-headed; and if the idea of European unity
has attracted, outside its institutions, an extremist and sometimes
lunatic fringe, even the Commonwealth, after all, has its League
of Empire Loyalists. It is very rare indeed to hear militancy of
this kind expressed by "Eurocrats". For many of them, indeed,
one of the attractions of their task is that it seems to promise a
practical alternative to sabre-rattling, by meeting Communist
challenges on the economic plane.

In this respect, perhaps, there is therefore a closer analogy with
the agelong quest for perpetual peace. The Schuman Declaration
of 1950 which originally proposed the Coal and Steel Community
began with the assertion that "world peace can only be safeguarded by creative efforts which match the dangers that threaten

it". One immediate aim, in this context, was to make a future war between France and Germany impossible by pooling their basic heavy industries. In 1950, with World War II only five years back, the possibility of such a war seemed less remote than it does now; but if even then the real dangers lay elsewhere, this limitation of aim at least proved that the Schuman Plan was no Kantian dream : it at least sighted a target within range. Many Europeans feel, moreover, that a united Western Europe stands a better chance of safeguarding world peace than a Europe divided by nationalism. Some have even hoped that the lessons and methods of European integration may one day be applied in a wider world.

If the hope of peace, then, is something that the European Community shares with its forebears, the same is true of "cosmopolitanism". Not since the eighteenth century, perhaps, has Western Europe enjoyed so high a degree of cultural unity, even uniformity. In large measure this is a general phenomenon, hastened by better communications, the growth of travel, the learning of languages, the spread of translations, the increase of trade, the advance of mechanization. It would have happened whatever the fate of plans for a European Community. All airports look alike, and most new cities look like Düsseldorf. As if alarmed by a prospect that their own efforts are bringing marginally nearer, the protagonists of European integration have repeatedly gone on record to the effect that they only wish to unite Europe, not to make it uniform. In the event, both natural conservatism and human contrariness will probably postpone the steel-and-concrete utopia long enough for our descendants to find its present manifestations quaintly old-fashioned, like the *Bauhaus*. *"Mir woelle bleiwe wat mir sin"* ("We want to stay as we are") runs the national motto of Luxembourg, that repeatedly invaded Grand Duchy; and it is characteristic of this spirit that in 1957-8, just when the Rome Treaties were beginning to mark yet another stage on the way to an integrated Europe, the French street names in the Luxembourg capital were supplemented by translations in the national tongue, Letzeburgesch, of which the motto above is a fair sample. There seems no reason to believe that Luxembourgers are alone in their resistance to *Gleichschaltung*.

This question of what might be called "States' Rights" recalls the much quoted analogy with the United States. In some respects, this has been fruitful for the Community, not only as a readily understood model for its own institutional structure—with Executive, Parliament, and Supreme Court—but also in securing United States support for a project that seemed like a foreign production of Scenes From Early American History. Jean Monnet's *Les Etats-Unis d'Europe ont commencé* has already been mentioned: it is no coincidence that Monnet is much admired in America. Professor Hallstein, too, has in several policy speeches made close comparisons between the Common Markets of the European Community and of the United States; and Community experts have consulted American experience when formulating their own ideas on both anti-trust policy and inter-State transport rules. In some respects, indeed, the analogy is suggestive: but Hallstein himself is the first to admit, if pressed, that it may sometimes be facile. In language, history, tradition, and degree of industrial development, the Community's member states are very different from the founder States of the American Union, and the world they inhabit is different too. Nevertheless, the American ideal has a potency in continental Europe that it no doubt lacks in Great Britain; and imperfect historical parallels, as history itself shows, are among the commonest motives for revolutionary action.

Another such parallel, once allegedly quoted by the British Prime Minister, is that between the European Community and the Napoleonic Empire. This, I think, is in some ways more misleading than that with the United States. It is true that Napoleon's conquests helped to free Europe from some of its former territorial divisions, from some of the relics of feudalism, and from a number of tariff barriers inside national borders; it is true that they also left indestructible traces of French laws, institutions, and administrative methods, as well as a system of weights and measures for which continental schoolchildren should never cease to be grateful. But the essential feature of this transformation was its accomplishment by force. In the present European Community, it is true that French is *de facto* the main working language, despite the official status of German, Italian, and Dutch; it is true that France first proposed the Schuman Plan, and that she has often had her way in subsequent developments, many of which evince the characteristics of Gallic administrative skill. It is true, too, that President de Gaulle reputedly regards the Community as an instrument of French European policy. But this interpretation, although flattering to the Quai d'Orsay, would be hotly contested by the *Auswärtige Amt*, to say nothing of the Foreign Offices of other Member States. Skilful diplomacy can do a great deal, but it can hardly be compared to armed conquest. And as one watches at close hand the mysterious workings of the Community, they begin to look rather like the movements of a planchette at a séance, where each participant is pushing, perhaps believing that he can control the operation, but in fact producing, with his partners round the table, results that none could achieve alone and that even the assembled company could not accomplish without the planchette.

"Supranational" is no better a description of this process than "supernatural"; but federalists and internationalists generally have certainly contributed in very large measure to the success of the European Community. A recent Oxford historian of the movement has astutely pointed out that "because in their preoccupation with ultimate aims many federalists were classified as starry-eyed, British observers were tempted to write off the federalists on the continent as equally cranky and unrepresenta-

tive".[26] True enough, some of them are : but federalist leanings
are shared by many who would be impatient with federalist
ideology : it is convenient to call them "Europeans", in quotation
marks, as indeed they are called on the continent. "Europeans"
in this sense include members of all political parties except the
extreme Right and the Communists; and prominent among them
are not only the Catholics mentioned already, but also trade
unionists and Socialists. In this sense the non-Communist Left in
Europe has returned to its earlier traditions. An English trade
unionist who has studied this aspect of the question in great detail
has stated categorically that "the trade unions, in most cases,
have been among the keenest and most consistent supporters of
integration projects in Western Europe, and are in large part
responsible for the broadly based and positive support the Communities have".[27] The unions' chief complaint, indeed, is that
integration has not gone far enough. It was European Socialists,
likewise, who in 1947 in London founded the International
Study and Action Committee for the Socialist United States of
Europe, later transformed into the still active Socialist Movement
for the United States of Europe. Paul-Henri Spaak, the Belgian
Socialist, gave his name to the "Spaak Report" from which the
Common Market and Euratom Treaties were evolved. Another,
Paul Finet, formerly first President of the International Confederation of Free Trade Unions, later became President of the
E.C.S.C. High Authority, of which he is still a Member. If both
are now comparatively moderate Socialists, the same cannot be
said of some of their party colleagues, who are among the most
active and vocal Members of the European Parliament, having
learned—perhaps from Communist tactics—a lesson also consistently applied by "Europeans" in general : that one way of
achieving a position of influence is to be the hardest-working and
best-briefed member of a heterogeneous team. If, as a later
chapter will attempt to show, the economic theory and practice
of European integration is not that of classical *dirigisme* or full

central planning, it is partly thanks to the efforts of European
Socialists that it is equally distinct from pure *laissez-faire*
capitalism and Manchester-school Free Trade.

In sum, then, the European Community, like all institutions, is
a complex creation which bears many different traces of its past.
But among its more immediate origins there is at least one new
element that distinguishes it from those fragments of its pre-
history considered hitherto. Most previous plans for European
unity found their *raison d'être* within Europe : many of them,
for instance, sought only to put an end to Europe's squabbles. In
one sense, some of them were really plans for a new universal
order, limited to Europe only because their authors regarded
Europe as the main part of the world. This was a conviction that
could hardly survive World War II. As the smoke cleared and
Europeans began to rebuild their ruined cities, an additional,
external reason for European unity forced itself on their attention. It became clear that the world as a whole had been dras-
tically re-oriented by the emergence of two super-powers, with
the prospect of a third in the Far East. The European balance
of power gave place to the world balance of terror; and Europe,
once the world's focus, seemed in danger of becoming its cockpit
or its Balkans. Here was a challenge of scale. What it meant in
terms of politics was suddenly, dramatically obvious; but its
economic causes had already been maturing in the years before
World War II.

CHAPTER III

THE ECONOMIC BACKGROUND

Economics and politics are the seamy sides of one another, if only in the sense that any distinction between them is a matter of convenience rather than conviction. With this proviso in mind, it is perhaps worth while to trace the economic background of some of the political changes referred to in the previous chapter. In the process, two main themes will emerge—on the one hand, the transformation of Europe's relative position in the world; on the other, the parallel transformation of the classical theory of free trade and the growth of theories of "the larger market". Without undue violence to chronology, the story may be divided into three stages: the first, that of European expansion and the popularity of free trading; the second, that of "the end of the frontier" in colonial development, and the consequent exacerbation of economic nationalism; and the third, that of Europe's relative economic decline and the new application of theories of the larger market.

Although the Industrial Revolution had already had some important effects by the early years of the nineteenth century, Europe's most rapid industrial expansion came in the middle years of the century with the building of the railways, which helped eliminate geographical barriers to trade. This, like previous industrialization, spread at an uneven pace, with Western Europe in the lead, Central Europe some way behind, and Eastern Europe lagging further still.

Great Britain, already far advanced in the cotton industry, was by 1850 producing some fifty million tons of coal and nearly half the world's pig iron : she was not only "the workshop of the world" but also its leading trader, shipper, and banker. Belgium followed only a little way behind her in making a start on railway development, and was ahead of her in having a national railway policy; until the 1860's, indeed, Belgium was the only continental power to keep pace with Britain even on a smaller scale. France, with greater self-sufficiency in agriculture, developed more gradually, building her first major railway only in 1837, seven years after Britain and two years after Belgium; but she saw an almost equally rapid accumulation of her industrial population in a few large towns, and—beginning in 1864 with the *Comité des Forges*—a concentration of her heavy industries into large family groupings. In Germany, on the other hand, although her mineral resources matched Great Britain's, industrial development was hampered at first by political divisions; but partly for this reason, the impact of the railways, which first began in 1835, was eventually even more dramatic. Italy's economic development was likewise retarded by political disunity—and political preoccupations—in the early years of the century; while Austro-Hungary and Russia lagged still further behind.

A counterpart to these differences between European nations was the complicated pattern of their colonial development. Here too, Britain was in the lead. Her old colonial Empire was centred chiefly in North America, in Canada and the Caribbean, with strong residual connections in the United States : it gradually extended to India, Ceylon, Burma, Australasia, and the South Pacific, as well as West and South Africa. France, stripped of some of her older colonies, spread her influence chiefly in tropical and sub-tropical regions—Algeria, Syria, West and Equatorial Africa, Indo-China, and Tahiti; while the Netherlands retained the Dutch East Indies. But despite this diversity, an overall pattern was emerging in which western and northern Europe, together with the eastern United States, began to rely on southern and eastern Europe, on western and southern America, and even on Australasia and India, for industrial raw materials and for food to meet the needs of increasing populations at home. The scene was thus set for moves towards freer trade; and here once again Great Britain led the way, not so much for ideological reasons as because of her economic position and her growing dependence on world commerce.

The ideal of free trade was one that had already inspired enthusiasm towards the end of the eighteenth century. In the late 1770's Adam Smith had devoted Book IV of *The Wealth of Nations* to a sustained attack on its mercantilist opponents; and in the 1780's Sir John Sinclair, in an otherwise sober *History of the Public Revenue*, had exclaimed: "My breast glows at the idea that a time may possibly soon arrive when the ships of Denmark, of Sweden, and of Russia, of Holland, of Austria, of France itself, and of Great Britain shall no longer be debarred from sailing to the coasts of Chili and of Peru, or be precluded by any proud monopolist from exchanging the commodities of Europe for the riches of America; and when every state, in proportion to the fertility of its soil, and to the industry of its inhabitants, may be certain of procuring all the necessaries and the conveniences of life."[1]

Similar visions were to be invoked by the Anti-Corn Law League of 1839; but just as the original establishment of the Corn Laws was partly an acknowledgment that British agriculture needed protection, so their repeal in 1846, together with the abolition of the restrictive Navigation Laws three years later, amounted to an admission that Britain was becoming a predominantly industrial power. Not only could a growing population no longer be fed only by a comparatively static agricultural economy, but British manufacturers and merchants were anxious to face European competition which they knew they could easily beat. It was significant, indeed, that for some years, while Britain adopted a free trading policy, other European countries remained deliberately protectionist. Their reason was explained at the time by the German economist Friedrich List : nations, he said, "must modify their systems according to the measure of their own progress." In the early phases, they would adopt free trade with more advanced nations as a means of raising themselves from a primitive state and of developing their agriculture; in the next they would require protection for their growing industries; and only in the final stage, at the peak of their industrial development, would they revert to free trade.[2]

Not before 1860, in fact, was there any move towards free trade among continental nations. In that year, the Cobden Treaty brought about a reduction of French duties on coal and most manufactures in return for a lower British tariff on wine and brandy. Similar Treaties followed with Belgium, Germany, Italy, Switzerland, Norway, Spain, the Netherlands, and Austria. It was no coincidence, however, that this same period was one of general industrial growth in Europe. One index of it was a further expansion of the railways. By 1870, almost all European countries had respectable railway networks, and between 1870 and 1890 their mileage was doubled in France, Italy, and Switzerland, and nearly doubled in Belgium, the Netherlands, and Spain.

The same period, moreover, saw the achievement of Italian and German unification. Cavour, the Piedmontese architect of Italian unity, had made his own fortune by mechanizing the farming of his family estate. Once in power, he sought to apply similar methods to Italy. In Germany, railway development had gone far enough by 1860 to make it possible to tap vast resources of coal and lignite, bringing output to a level higher than that of Belgium and France. After 1871, the *Reichsbank* helped Germany to wield formidable financial influence; and in the years that followed she developed into a net food importer and a major industrial power—not only in the field of electricity and chemicals which she had made her own, but also in what had once been Britain's traditional preserves of coal, iron, and shipping.

This vast and rapid economic growth disturbed the old equilibrium in Europe and led to both economic and political tension.
In 1879 Bismarck had already led the way back to protectionist
policies by imposing tariffs; France did likewise throughout the
1880's, and Great Britain followed suit : the result was a general
European movement away from free trade. "Circumstances have
so far changed," wrote William Cunningham in 1882, "and our
industrial rivals have so far developed in efficiency and in commercial influence, that the question is forced upon public attention whether it is prudent for us to trust entirely to *laissez faire*,
or whether we are not compelled to take active measures to retain
and extend the market for our goods."[3] Marketing, indeed, was
becoming a problem. If the nineteenth century had seen the cul-
mination of the producers' economy, with attention concentrated
on the problems and means of production, the turn of the century
witnessed the beginnings of a consumer economy, with attention
focused on the finding of markets for goods. This, together with
the quest for fresh capital outlets and further raw materials—to
say nothing of emigration, exploring and missionary zeal, and
European suspicion and rivalry—was among the reasons for the
extraordinary race for new colonies that marked the close of the
nineteenth century. In 1875, less than one-tenth of Africa had
been appropriated : twenty years later, only one-tenth remained
independent. Between 1871 and 1900, Great Britain acquired an
extra $4\frac{1}{4}$ million square miles of colonial territory, France $3\frac{1}{2}$
million, and Russia half a million. At the same time, Germany
secured an Empire of one million square miles, Belgium 900,000,
and Italy 185,000. By 1900, in the rather lofty words of a standard history of the period, "nearly all the waste spaces had
already been staked out."[4] As a later historian put it : "The
beginning of the twentieth century brought not only the 'end of
the frontier' in American history; it brought a limit to the expansion of the world's colonial frontiers in general and forced the

powers back upon their more dangerous rivalries in Europe."[5] The second stage of the present story—the stage of economic nationalism—had already begun; and one of its major landmarks was the 1914–18 War.

The financial expense involved in that war has been estimated at £45 thousand million: but its economic cost was literally incalculable. It included not only widespread physical ruin, but also lasting damage to Europe's economic system and more especially, perhaps, to its ability to come to terms with new economic facts.

The material destruction wrought by the war was comparatively quickly patched up. The initial stages were slow and painful; but the very magnitude of the task, with immense demand for food and building, and a huge ex-Service labour force to be re-absorbed, helped to trigger off the boom of 1919 and 1920. By 1921, despite a temporary recession and a slower rate of recovery in Eastern Europe, the world's productive capacity was back at a level that might have been forecast in 1913.

Much of this capacity, however, as will be seen later, now lay outside Europe. What was more, Europe's own economic system had undergone some changes. Not only had victorious nationalism, especially in the Balkans, proved to be wedded to ideals of self-sufficiency, preferring tariff protection to the old hope of freer trade: the Western European nations themselves emerged from the war with a far greater degree of economic separatism. Many of them had perforce adopted what in Germany was known as *Kriegswirtschaft* (a war economy), of which one significant feature was the development of *ersatz* or synthetic substances, such as plastics, to replace—and later in some cases to supersede—imported raw materials. This, together with the remnants of *Kriegssozialismus*—greater centralization and increased state intervention in economic affairs—helped to make Europe's economic life between the two world wars very different from what it had been in the early years of the century.

But the most decisive change in Europe's economic position was the fact that it emerged from the war as a debtor continent; and the response of statesmen to the whole question of war debts and reparations, often under popular or demagogic pressure, showed that old habits of thought were still being applied to a totally new situation. Following Lord Keynes's masterly and scathing analysis of *The Economic Consequences of the Peace*,[6] many pens have described what Sir Winston Churchill later called the "sad story of complicated idiocy"[7] that condemned Germany to paying reparations which in the form of goods would have dislocated industry in the recipient countries, and in the form of cash could only be supplied by vast, continued, and virtually unrepayable loans from the United States, to whom the recipients of German reparations then returned a sizeable proportion of their spoils in settlement of their own debts. Attempts to break out of this financial game of rounders met such responses as President Calvin Coolidge's "They hired the money, didn't they?" By a doubly false analogy, money was being treated as if it were wealth, and nations as if they were private individuals settling their debts within a stable economic and monetary system. But, as Churchill observed, "payments which are only the arbitrary, artificial transmission across the exchange of such very large sums as arise in war finance cannot fail to derange the whole process of world economy".[8] When in 1923 France occupied the Ruhr to enforce reparation payments, the German Mark collapsed—and was pushed—under a flood of recklessly printed paper money, which made nonsense of reparation accounting, enriched speculators overnight, and at the same time ruined the *rentier* classes, helping to pave the way for National Socialism.

Meanwhile, another catastrophe was in preparation elsewhere, also partly a consequence of the post-war game of rounders. As a debtor, Europe now needed to export more in order to pay her way. Her chief creditor was the United States; and the most satisfactory way for her debts to be settled would have been for her to sell in the American market. The United States, however, rich in natural resources and in industrial capacity, had little need or taste for imports, and maintained a high tariff. Unless Europe's exports could earn large sums outside the United States, therefore, she had either to borrow or to pay from her own depleted reserves of gold. In an insecure world, new loans tended to be more expensive and of shorter duration. Lending money became more lucrative and therefore more speculative: high rates of interest and the prospect of quick returns tempted away capital that might have been productively invested in Europe. Payment from reserves, on the other hand, meant that the bulk of the world's gold went where it was not needed—into United States vaults; and since by 1925 most countries had returned to the gold standard or the gold exchange standard, this already meant that prices were tending to fall as gold became more scarce. More important still, production in both the United States and Europe was rising at a time when it was growing more difficult to pay for it: and in 1926 American agricultural and raw materials prices both began to slacken. This, in conjunction with the fantastically over-optimistic speculation spree on Wall Street, led to the inevitable crash in 1929, when share prices collapsed with an echo that resounded throughout the world.

In its dimensions, its causes, and its effects, the 1929 slump was unlike any of the previous crises and depressions that had occurred at roughly ten-year intervals since 1818. If its causes were various, so were the measures adopted to meet it. Some of them were measures of purely national economic defence—state control of currency and exchange rates, the raising of protective tariffs, the quantitative restriction of imports. Others were regional remedies, such as the formation of the Oslo Group, the agreement between agricultural producers in Eastern Europe, or the Ottawa Agreements of 1932, whereby Great Britain systematized and consolidated Imperial Preference. Others again were attempts at widespread collective action, such as the 1932 Lausanne Convention which ended reparations, and the World Economic Conference of 1933. What all these steps had in common was that they led further away from the pre-war world of *laisserfaire* and freer trade; and if some of them moved towards greater economic nationalism, others pointed in a very different direction. The second stage of the present story was coming to an end. What had hastened it was the change in Europe's position in the world.

World War I had already made that change dramatic. Absent for four years from peaceful productive pursuits, Europe found at the end of the war that others had begun to fill her place. Not until 1929, in fact, did she seem to be recovering her pre-war share of total world production; and even this recovery did not last. In 1913, Europe West of the Oder had produced 45 per cent of the world's industrial goods. By 1937, the percentage had dropped to 34, and was still falling.

This was partly due, of course, to the growing industrialization of hitherto backward countries outside Europe. Such a process of "catching up" had been inevitable ever since the 1850's and '60's, when Europeans had financed the first railways in South America and Asia: it had already begun during World War I, and was hastened by the 1929 crisis. So far, however, the growth of the developing countries still lagged miserably behind Europe's, and was only a very minor factor in the world scale.

A second factor which was ultimately to have dramatic effects on the relative status of Western Europe was the growth of Soviet Russia. In the past, Russia too had lagged behind; but signs of change were already apparent towards the end of the nineteenth century. Serfdom had been abolished; and between 1891 and 1905 the road to future progress had been opened by the completion of the 3,800-mile Siberia railway. Russian losses in the war, although three times those of France, had had a smaller relative impact on her vast population; and in post-Revolutionary Russia, the First Five-Year Plan in 1928 was the herald of her later dizzy growth. Between 1929 and 1937, Russian crude steel production more than trebled : by the end of World War II, the Soviet Union and her satellites had become an industrial giant. In the years between the wars, however, it was Russia's growth rate rather than the scale of her industrial production that dazzled the onlooker; but if this could partly be ascribed to ruthless planning and direction of resources, the same could not be said of the similar rapid growth recorded by North American industry.

America's industrial growth, indeed, was the most important quantitative factor in changing the pattern of world production between the wars. While Europe's share of total industrial output dwindled, that of North America as a whole not only caught up but even began to overtake it, rising from 36.5 per cent in 1913 to 42.1 per cent in 1929. By 1938, while industrial production in Great Britain, France, and Belgium stood respectively 54 per cent, 77 per cent and 79 per cent higher than in 1900, the comparable figure for the United States was 163 per cent. In Europe, only Germany, Italy and Sweden could match or outstrip the United States' growth rate, and no country could equal Canada's: in terms of absolute production figures, even Germany came well behind the United States. Moreover, despite the comparatively small proportion of North American products sold for export, these relative changes were also reflected in the trade figures. Between 1928 and 1938, total world trade contracted sharply : but while North American exports dropped from $6.9 thousand million to 4.1, and imports from 6.0 to 3.1, Europe's exports fell from $14.2 thousand million to 6.6, and her imports from 18.2 to 7.8—both absolutely and relatively a much greater decline.

Among the explanations suggested to account for this disparity between American and European development, the size of the United States market was one that caught the attention of Europeans. As two astute commentators have put it, "The moment when the 'American era' began is significant : it coincides with the beginning of the process of disintegration in the world economy. While the American economy could develop on the basis of a single market of continental proportions, in Europe the advent of economic nationalism disturbed the multilateral equilibrium of international trade."[9] Obviously, other factors played a part of the story, and it would be naïve to presuppose a simple correlation between the size of the market and the rate of economic growth. But at a time when a return to free trade was clearly out of the question, Europeans certainly began to wonder whether they might not rival American prosperity if they could establish in their own continent a market of American size.

The basic idea, of course, was as old as the philosophy of free trade itself. Adam Smith had long ago stated that "the division of labour is limited by the extent of the market";[10] and the arguments for large markets were substantially those of the classical economists. Catering for a large market, they pointed out, would make possible economies of scale in mass production and distribution, resulting in lower costs; large-scale producers would have easier access to sources of capital, bigger research and training budgets, better planning facilities and therefore greater stability. Competition in a wider area would stimulate technical improvement and modernization, and would lead to the survival of the fittest; while this in turn would encourage greater specialization among firms and regions, so that industries would be more economically located and each would concentrate upon what it could do best.

Stated thus baldly, the classical doctrine is crudely liberal and even rather brutal : but it makes some sense. Indeed, although early instances of larger markets added new elements to the old free-trading philosophy, they nevertheless lent colour to its general thesis. The suppression of internal economic barriers in France, the United Kingdom, and the Swiss Confederation undoubtedly made for greater prosperity, as it did in the U.S.A. The spread of the railways in Europe, creating larger markets by reducing travel costs, was an even more striking instance of the same process; and the *Zollverein* in nineteenth-century Germany, which gradually united into a single market a number of small principalities which hitherto had been divided by innumerable customs tariffs, laid the foundations, for over a century of rapid economic growth.

At the same time, however, experience also suggested that the pure gospel of free trade stood in need of revision. This was due partly to practical changes in economic society, and partly to a growing sophistication of economic theory. Chief among the practical changes were the greater responsibilities of the state in economic affairs and the greater size and complexity of modern industry. On the one hand, the state's activities not only embraced such matters as labour laws, welfare projects, and indirect restraint or stimulus by means of taxes and tax reliefs, subsidies, marketing organizations, and monetary controls, but also direct participation in the economy itself. By 1955, indeed, the state's average current expenditure in Western Europe represented 28 per cent of the gross national product; and government ownership or participation affected central banks, railways, airlines, electricity, coalmining, oil, steel, transport equipment, and chemicals—to name only the most important industrial sectors.[11] On the other hand, the nature of modern technology and modern finance had led to the formation, in all European countries, of industrial units and groupings far larger than any imagined by Adam Smith. Many of them—Siemens, I.C.I., Fiat, Unilever, Arbed, Sidelor, Brufina—are national household words; and many too have international ramifications.

Partly because of this altered context, moreover, classical economic theory had undergone drastic modifications, symbolized and in some degree accomplished by the so-called "Keynesian

revolution". One of the essential elements of this revolution was
its abandonment of the notion that a modern economy can rely
on some quasi-automatic and self-regulating mechanism of prices
and interests—what Adam Smith called "an invisible hand".
While different Governments are pledged in theory to different
degrees of "liberalism" or "planning", all in practice exercise a
variety of controls, replacing the hidden hand by measures
intended at most to ensure steady social and regional development and at least to iron out the cyclical booms and recessions
which although still intractable are no longer accepted as
inevitable. If economics was once little more than natural
history, it is now coming more and more to resemble applied
biology.] *It was never the first & ought not be the second*

It is in taking account of these developments that theories of
the larger market differ from classical theories of free trade. Free
trade, like patriotism, is "not enough". The full implications of
this change only emerged from practice in the moves towards
economic integration in Europe which followed World War II;
but some of them were already being expressed between the wars.
As early as 1915, indeed, when the German theorist Friedrich
Naumann proposed a customs union with Austria in his influential book *Mitteleuropa*, he argued : "No European nation, not
even the German, by itself is large enough for an economic state
of world standing. This is the result of the capitalist economic
system. This economic state has its customs frontiers just as the
military state has its trenches. Within these frontiers it tries to
create a universally active exchange area. This involves an economic legislation, while advising the national governments on the
remainder. The direct functions of the economic government
include customs, cartel regulations, export arrangements, patent
laws, protection of trade marks, control of raw materials, etc. Its
indirect sphere of activity includes commercial legislation, social
welfare and many other things."[12] In 1939, detailed study of the
Zollverein led another writer to the similar conclusion that a

customs union—one form of regional free trade or larger market —"can seldom be regarded as a permanent arrangement. Its members must sooner or later decide if they are to go backwards or forwards. If they go back they revert to their old position as independent tariff units. If they go forward they unify their economic organizations as far as possible. Common tariffs are followed by common systems of internal taxation—the same excises, the same direct taxes, the same monopolies. They adopt the same weights and measures, the same coinage, the same railway tariffs, the same code of commercial and maritime law, the same legislation with regard to the regulation of industry and workers".[13]

The most complete expression of this line of thought, however, is to be found in a League of Nations study on customs unions, republished in 1947 by the United Nations. It declared : "For a customs union to exist, it is necessary to allow free movement of goods within the union. For a customs union to be a reality it is necessary to allow free movement of persons. For a customs union to be stable it is necessary to maintain free exchangeability of currency and stable exchange rates within the union. This implies, *inter alia*, free movement of capital within the union. When there is free movement of goods, persons, and capital in any area, diverse economic policies concerned with maintaining economic activity cannot be pursued. To assure uniformity of policy, some political mechanism is required. The greater the interference of the state in economic life, the greater must be the political integration within a customs union."[14]

The cat was out of the bag at last. The theory of larger markets and customs unions led directly to the problem of political union. It was significant, indeed, that all the historical examples of larger markets—in France, in the United Kingdom, in Switzerland, in the German *Zollverein*, in Italy, and in the United States —had been preceded, accompanied, or followed, by pressure for political as well as economic integration. In the words of a young

French economist deeply involved in the operations of the Common Market, "Political union by itself soon proves impracticable without a corresponding economic union; economic union is only feasible if the states—or one of them—include it in their political programme".[15] If the Keynesian revolution had thus in some sort remarried economics and politics, the history of Europe after World War II was to prove that the union was fertile.

CHAPTER IV

THE POST-WAR DEBATE

WORLD WAR II and its aftermath strengthened both the political and the economic arguments for greater unity among nations. On both fronts there was widespread determination to avoid previous mistakes. For a short honeymoon period, it was hoped that unity could be achieved on the scale of world politics. This proved an illusion. Meanwhile, the re-shaping of the world's economy seemed the next most urgent task. But, as time went on, it was within Western Europe that the major effort had to be concentrated, politically as well as economically; and even here there were contrasting views of what was needed and what was possible.

Ideas about European unity had by no means been dormant during the war of 1939-45. Particularly in America, refugees such as Count Coudenhove-Kalergi and Don Luigi Sturzo had helped to keep interest in the subject alive. In Europe itself in 1940, at the suggestion of Jean Monnet, then in London to co-ordinate supplies and armaments, Winston Churchill had proposed Franco-British union and joint nationality; and three years later, in March 1943, he broadcast an appeal for a postwar "Council of Europe". In the same year, the French statesman René Mayer had suggested to General de Gaulle the idea of an economic federation of Europe—an idea which may have inspired de Gaulle's subsequent proposal of "a strategic and economic federation between France, Belgium, Luxembourg, and the Netherlands, a federation to which Great Britain might adhere". Pope Pius XII meanwhile was thinking in terms of a "close union of the European states inspired by Catholicism—Germany, France, Italy, Spain, Belgium, Portugal"; but the notion of some future European grouping was not confined to Catholics. In July 1944, after a secret meeting in Geneva in May, members of the Resistance movement of all shades of political opinion and many creeds affirmed in a joint declaration that "Federal Union alone could ensure the preservation of liberty and civilization on the Continent of Europe, bring about economic recovery and enable the German people to play a peaceful rôle in European affairs". In March 1945, at a public meeting in Paris, the first steps were taken to form what later became the European Union of Federalists. At the same time, the postwar Constitutions of France and Italy—and subsequently that of the German Federal Republic—all contained clauses envisaging future limitations on national sovereignty. At the end of the war, indeed, many Europeans were thinking, like General de Gaulle, of some kind of "association between Slavs, Germans, Gauls, and Latins" to restore stability in Europe.[1]

The inclusion of "Slavs" in this list was significant: for the first years after World War II were in fact occupied with the search for a much wider unity than that of Western Europe. In England, not long had elapsed since popular dance bands had been playing songs like "Russian Rose"; in France, the copy of André Malraux's Spanish War film, L'Espoir, in the Paris Cinémathèque was prefaced with a Ministerial tribute to France's Communist allies; and in fact there were Communist Ministers in the early postwar Governments of France, Italy, and Belgium. In the wider world, beginning in 1941 with the Atlantic Charter, and continuing in 1942 with the Declaration of the United Nations which led successively to the Dumbarton Oaks Conference of 1944, and to the Yalta and San Francisco meetings of 1945, the wartime allies laid the bases of the United Nations Organization that was to supersede—and, it was hoped, improve upon—the League of Nations in Geneva. The U.N. differed from

its predecessor in that this time the United States and the Soviet
Union were members from the start, and that the Assembly,
which enjoyed a little more power than before, could take
decisions by a two-thirds majority vote instead of only unanimously, as had been the case with most important decisions of the
League.

It was not long, however, before these early postwar hopes
were punctured. The Council of the United Nations, this time
called the Security Council, was composed partly of five permanent members—Nationalist China, France, the U.K., the U.S.A.,
and the U.S.S.R.—and partly of six other states elected in two-
year rotation; but on all but procedural matters it was handicapped by the fact that each of the permanent members enjoyed
the right of veto. Within four years, the Soviet Union was to use
this right thirty times. For many people, indeed, the familiar
Soviet veto became the symbol of postwar cleavage between
East and West; but this was only the most publicised of the
growing difficulties. Even in the wartime Resistance movements,
such Communist contingents as—in France—the *Franc-tireur et
partisan* group had frequently clashed with their "bourgeois"
comrades; and even while the United Nations Organization was
being established, the first peace talks showed, in the words of
one disillusioned reporter, that "the Russians regard international
conferences as opportunities for the recognition of situations
which have already been created by the exercise of power, not as
occasions for the negotiation of reasonable settlements mutually
acceptable".[2]

When V. M. Molotov, the Soviet Foreign Minister, met Ernest
Bevin, the British Foreign Secretary, and James Byrnes, the
American Secretary of State, in London in September 1945, he
made it clear that Russia had no intention of relinquishing her
de facto grip on Eastern Europe: he was no doubt encouraged
in his firmness by President Roosevelt's Yalta statement that
American troops could not be expected to stay in Europe for

more than two years after the war. The same Russian attitude was confirmed in the talks held in Paris and New York during the following year, when the pro-Soviet states all took a similar line, particularly in advocating large-scale reparations and opposing the attempt to make Trieste a free port and the Danube and Black Sea open international waterways. In Austria, the Soviet Union resisted until 1955 any peace treaty which by ending the four-power occupation would have deprived her of continued spoils in the form of oil and capital goods from the Soviet zone. In Germany, although she agreed at the end of 1946 to discuss plans for economic union among the four occupation zones, the basic situation established by Russia's successful race for Berlin in 1945 has continued to this day.

Winston Churchill's speech of March 1946 in Fulton, Missouri, was one of the first public acknowledgments of the way events were moving. To many hopeful people it came as a shock : but the sobering evidence continued to pile up. Late in 1946, the Greek civil war, endemic since 1943, was revived in a new offensive led by General Vafiades and equipped through neighbouring Communist countries. In March 1947, President Harry S. Truman responded with the "Truman Doctrine", a promise to aid resistance to armed aggression or subversion—in this case with a $400 million appropriation for Greece and Turkey. During the next three months, Communist Ministers were excluded from the Governments of Belgium, France, and Italy : non-Communists were likewise excluded from those of Eastern Europe. On October 5 came the creation in Belgrade of the Communist Information Bureau, or Cominform, whose aim was to co-ordinate Communist activities not only in Eastern Europe, but also in Italy and France, where the Party enjoyed a substantial number of Parliamentary seats and—until the breakaway of non-Communist trade unions—effective control of much of organized labour. During the hard winter of 1947-8, indeed,

Communist influence was active, although not decisive, in the organization of waves of industrial strikes.

Meanwhile, on October 9, 1947, Moscow had published the "Zhdanov Manifesto", accusing the United States of imperialist and warlike intentions. Four months later, in February, 1948, came the Communist coup in Prague which added Czechoslovakia to a list of Soviet "satellites" already comprising Jugoslavia, Rumania, Bulgaria, Poland, and Hungary. In March, Great Britain, France, Belgium, the Netherlands, and Luxembourg signed the Brussels Treaty to promise each other all possible military aid in the event of armed attack in Europe. Not for nothing did this come to be called "Western Union". Unlike the Dunkirk Treaty concluded by France and Britain the year before, it was no longer limited to defence against Germany, and was thus the first post-war Treaty to recognize the potential danger from Soviet military power. In June, moreover, the situation became more tense still. In reaction to the joint currency reform in the three Western zones of Germany, Russia imposed her land blockade on the city of Berlin : it was only removed after Britain and the United States had by-passed it for nearly eleven months with an airlift of supplies and even raw materials. Before the end of the blockade, in April, 1949, the United States, Canada, and Norway joined the Brussels Treaty powers in N.A.T.O., the North Atlantic Treaty Organization; and in the same year it became apparent that the Soviet Union possessed the atomic bomb. The honeymoon was over : the balance of terror had begun.

It was this sombre context that caused postwar attempts at political unity to be restricted to Western Europe. But it was not only in the political sphere that postwar efforts were perforce narrowed down from more global aspirations. For a variety of reasons, the same applied in the economic sphere as well.

In July, 1944, in a Conference at Bretton Woods, New Hampshire, forty-four of the wartime "United Nations" had met to seek ways of freeing and expanding international trade when the war was over. The outcome of their discussions was the establishment eighteen months later of two new institutions—the International Monetary Fund (I.M.F.) and the International Bank for Reconstruction and Development (I.B.R.D.), better known as the World Bank.[3] In so far as its aim was to promote world trade, the I.M.F. was essentially based on the notion that trade slows down because purchasing countries have no money left with which to pay for it. The purpose of the Fund was therefore to ease their problems by granting them credit, while at the same time exerting relentless pressure to force them back towards a satisfactory balance of payments. The World Bank, meanwhile, was to stimulate the necessary investments for rebuilding industries and economic infrastructures destroyed by the war, thus making possible the economic expansion which would be the basis for increased trade.

Even when it was set up in 1945, this double mechanism fell short of the hopes with which both Lord Keynes and the American Harry Dexter White had gone to Bretton Woods—that is, the creation of a world central bank to eliminate financial crises; and in practice, although it scored important successes, it also had serious limitations. The I.M.F., in particular, was limited not only by the economic conservatism of its underlying principle but also by its inability—and its members' reluctance—to exploit even a conservative philosophy by exerting more than mild and indirect pressure on its clients. The World Bank, on the other hand, represented a more radical approach to the problems of economic expansion : but it too has been criticized for acting on conservative banking principles and granting loans on its own capital instead of guaranteeing those raised on the ordinary capital market but earmarked for basic economic development with no prospect of immediate returns.

In these ways, therefore, the operations of the I.M.F. and the World Bank confirmed the beliefs of those who thought that more direct action was necessary to liberalize world trade. In 1946, the Economic and Social Committee of the United Nations Organization established a preparatory Committee to draw up an international trading code. This eventually saw the light as the Havana Charter, agreed by fifty-four states at a Conference in Havana from November, 1947 to March, 1948, and providing in particular for an International Trade Organization (I.T.O.). Unfortunately, the United States failed to ratify the Charter, and the I.T.O. never came into existence. As a result, the participating countries were forced back upon the General Agreement on Tariffs and Trade (G.A.T.T.), a looser interim arrangement negotiated in Geneva in the summer of 1947 while the abortive Havana Charter was being prepared.

G.A.T.T., while it has achieved a great deal as a code of good conduct and as a general forum for the discussion of world trade problems, has so far had less success than some had hoped as a means of achieving the liberalization and expansion of world trade. Among its handicaps have been the weak negotiating position of low-tariff countries, the difficulty of reducing the U.S. tariff, the problems of Commonwealth Preference, and the number of loopholes in the Agreement itself. Underlying a number of these difficulties, moreover, was the fact that like the I.M.F. and the World Bank, G.A.T.T. sought to tackle only one aspect of more general economic problems, and until 1951, at least, was chiefly concerned only with customs tariffs.

That postwar economic difficulties lay deeper than this was already becoming abundantly clear. Much, of course, had been achieved in the years immediately following the war. In Europe, such economic first-aid had been the work of U.N.R.R.A., the United Nations Relief and Rehabilitation Administration, set up in 1943. This gave aid without discrimination to occupied and defeated countries alike, and it extended to the East as well as the West. In 1946 it was replaced by the United Nations' Economic Commission for Europe (E.C.E.). Since this also enjoyed Russian participation, many believed that it might be able to bring about Europe-wide economic co-operation; but these hopes were clouded, if not dashed, by the unsuccessful and unhappy Moscow Conference of March and April, 1947. From that year onward, indeed, E.C.E. resigned itself to the real but much more modest tasks of helping to maintain a measure of East-West trade, providing a broad forum for general economic discussions, and preparing and presenting extremely useful technical and statistical information.

The decisive turning-point in the history of E.C.E. was probably the European economic crisis of 1947. When U.N.R.R.A. operations were ceasing, and Lend-Lease and the earliest postwar U.S. loans were exhausted, it quite suddenly became obvious how weak Western Europe's economy still was. The severe winter of 1946-47 threw this weakness into greater relief, with widespread unemployment and shortages, growing inflation, and a $7,000-million deficit on current account *vis-à-vis* the dollar area, 70 per cent of it towards the United States. It was in these circumstances, and against the background of increasing political difficulties with the Soviet Union, that General George Marshall, U.S. Secretary of State, announced on June 5, 1947, the American aid proposal that now bears his name. But this too was to be an instance of wider aims having to be narrowed down : for the offer of Marshall Aid was open also to the Soviet Union, who rejected it at the Paris Conference of July, 1947. Once again, the prospects of a general European settlement were receding; and once again the focus of endeavour was restricted by circumstances, not by choice.

Three basic ideas underlay the plan for Marshall Aid. The first was that there should be "a program", as General Marshall said, "designed to put Europe on its feet economically". The second was that this programme should be "designed by Europeans". The third was that it should be "a joint one, agreed to by a number, if not all European nations".[4] In other words, the United States was willing to help Europe to get on its feet again, but it wanted Europeans to replace the old anarchic system of their international economic relations by a system of co-operation, at the least. To that end, a Committee of European Economic Co-operation met in Paris and prepared first a report on Europe's needs and later a draft Convention for what became the 16- (and later 18-) nation O.E.E.C., the Organization for European Economic Co-operation, set up on April 16, 1948.

Within the limits imposed at the start by its members, the O.E.E.C. was to prove a remarkable economic success. By reducing quota restrictions on trade and comparing national economic policies, it assisted economic recovery over a broad area. By establishing a European Payments Union in which many intra-European debts could cancel each other out, it restrained the competitive scramble for scarce gold and dollars which had further hindered European trade. By encouraging the habit of consultation and co-operation in a number of different economic fields, it helped to achieve informal agreement which avoided many difficulties, and it undoubtedly paved the way for more ambitious ventures. Even within its own field, however, it suffered from certain limitations. Since much of its action was confined to the removal of quota restrictions, it did little to prevent the distortion or restraint of trade by other methods. In the domain of quotas, moreover, its method of liberalizing first one group of products and then another, rather than all together gradually, brought it up against a so-called "hard core" of difficult products which proved extremely intractable. Finally, it had more success in dealing with short-term difficulties than in tackling the longer-term problems of balanced growth, investment, and full employment.

One of the reasons for this was the limited scope and structure of the organization itself, which caused much debate both before and during its existence. When the Committee of European Economic Co-operation had first met in July, 1947, the American experts present, led by Under-Secretary William Clayton, had strongly urged the need not only for co-operation but for unity among the European participants. This aim was echoed in the policy statement of the United States' Economic Co-operation Act authorizing Marshall Aid, which recalled "the advantages which the United States has enjoyed through the existence of a large domestic market with no internal trade barriers", and affirmed the belief "that similar advantages can accrue to the countries of Europe". These words suggested something more like a customs union in Europe than a simple agreement to co-operate; and a former official of the U.S. State Department who was concerned with the matter has stated that it was "largely in response to American urging" that the Committee of European Economic Co-operation indeed discussed the possibility of a European customs union.[5] A smaller-scale model of such a union was gradually being established by Belgium, the Netherlands, and Luxembourg, who had signed the Benelux Convention on September 5, 1944; and Italy and France, in particular, were enthusiastic about the more extensive American proposal.[6] Great Britain, on the other hand, was not. After some discussion, the idea was finally buried in a 13-nation Customs Union Study Group; and the Economic Co-operation Act already quoted went on rather lamely, after its reference to "a large domestic market", to speak only of "economic co-operation", not of economic unity.[7]

Not only the scope, but also the structure of O.E.E.C. gave rise to debate at various times. At the March, 1948 meeting of the Committee of European Economic Co-operation, France sought to introduce a degree of "supranationality" into the future O.E.E.C. by giving it a strong executive board with a Secretary-General empowered to take major policy decisions of his own accord; but this suggestion, and the proposal for majority voting, met a cool reception from Great Britain, reluctant to give up the right of independent action, as well as from the Benelux countries, fearful of being overruled.[8] In the event, the O.E.E.C. became "first and foremost, a conference of sovereign states in permanent session" :[9] its executive body was a Council deciding by unanimous vote, but allowing dissentients to abstain without invalidating the decision of the remainder. In 1949 Mr. Paul Hoffman, first Administrator of the Economic Co-operation Act, sought to reinforce the Council by having it meet permanently, instead of occasionally, at Ministerial rather than official level : but this proposal, designed to save the time wasted by questions being referred back to Governments, encountered the objection that "divorced from their cabinet positions ministers had no independent authority or status".[10] Again in the following year the negotiation of the European Payments Union revealed a similar conflict of views over the degree of authority to be given to the Union's Managing Board. The United States' Economic Co-operation Administration had hoped to see this become a quasi-independent body with substantial power to influence national policies. Instead, under British and Scandinavian pressure, it was subordinated in practice to the O.E.E.C. Council and thus to the prior veto of any of the member states.

The first Secretary-General of the O.E.E.C., Robert Marjolin, now a Vice-President of the Common Market Commission, has pointed out that a broad similarity of outlook among members, the obvious need for action, and the effective rôle played by the Secretariat in fact made up for many of these structural weaknesses. "The right of veto," he concluded, "did not paralyse it, although it sometimes created difficulties."[11] Nevertheless, these conflicts of principle were important at the time, and the memory of them was to be important later. This was all the more so because the debates about the O.E.E.C. were echoed, much more publicly and bitterly, in a second Western European organization —the Council of Europe, set up on May 5, 1949.

The Council of Europe, although established after the O.E.E.C., was in fact the outcome of moves for political unity which had begun rather earlier. The original idea, as has been seen, had been mooted by Winston Churchill in a wartime broadcast on March 21, 1943; and it was he who most effectively revived it, in his now famous speech on September 19, 1946, at the University of Zurich. He declared:

"If Europe is to be saved from infinite misery, and indeed from final doom, there must be an act of faith in the European family and an act of oblivion against all the crimes and follies of the past. . . .

"What is this sovereign remedy? It is to recreate the European family, or as much of it as we can, and to provide it with a structure under which it can dwell in peace, safety, and freedom. We must build a kind of United States of Europe. . . ."[12]

These words fell on fertile soil. In the same year, a poll was conducted among 4,200 European parliamentarians, two-fifths of whom replied: of these, only 3 per cent were in principle opposed to federalism, and in France, Italy, Belgium, and the Netherlands more than half of the lower-house deputies favoured some form of European union.[13] Already, on May 16, 1946, the former Prime Minister of Belgium, Paul van Zeeland, had founded the European League for Economic Co-operation (E.L.E.C.). On December 15, the mainly left-wing European Union of Federalists was founded in Paris to group extensive national movements in Austria, Belgium, France, Germany, Greece, Italy, and Switzerland. At the beginning of 1947, Churchill himself organized the mainly right-wing United Europe Movement in Great Britain, while across the Channel the French Council for United Europe was set up to bring together parliamentary and governmental supporters of the movement from all parts of the political spectrum. In February, an international conference in London established the Socialist Movement for the United States of Europe, under the leadership of André Philip from France and Michel Rasquin (later to be a Member of the Common Market Commission) from Luxembourg; this had representatives also in Austria, Belgium, Germany, Great Britain, Greece, Italy, Spain, Switzerland, and the Scandinavian countries. June of the same year saw the formation of the *Nouvelles Equipes Internationales*, a largely Catholic and Franco-Belgian organization, as well as the first steps towards the creation two months later of the federalist *Europa-Bund* in Germany.[14]

The proliferation of these various groupings showed that support for "the European idea" came from all camps—clerical and anti-clerical, right and left, liberal and *dirigiste*, regionalist and multilateralist, "Atlantic" and "third force" : each felt that unity in Europe would give its own ideas greater scope. Behind these differences there were further latent contrasts, at least equally fundamental, between conflicting interpretations of the word "unity" itself. For the time being, however, it seemed more important to act together than to dispute the ultimate goal; and it was in an attempt to canalize varied currents of opinion that in December, 1947 there was set up the International Committee of the Movements for European Unity, which proceeded to organize the Congress of Europe held in The Hague from May 7 to 10, 1948. Subsequently, in October, the International Committee founded the "European Movement" as an umbrella organization for most of the existing "European" pressure groups. Only gradually did it become apparent that this was a multi-coloured umbrella with national panels of rather different hues.

The Hague Congress gathered together a remarkable concourse of more than 750 European statesmen, including Paul van Zeeland, Paul-Henri Spaak, Alcide de Gasperi, Georges Bidault, Léon Blum, Paul Ramadier, Paul Reynaud, and Robert Schuman. The British delegation was notable chiefly for its Conservative members, then out of office, including Churchill and his son-in-law Duncan Sandys. Among other things, the Congress called for political and economic union in Europe, a

European Assembly, and a European Court of Human Rights. There the matter might perhaps have rested had not the Europeans been invited to submit detailed plans for an Assembly to the members of the Brussels Treaty Organization, itself already pledged to promote economic, social, and cultural co-operation. In October, 1948 the Brussels powers set up a study commission under the presidency of Edouard Herriot, the veteran statesman who as Prime Minister of France in 1925 had been among the first to make an official appeal for a united Europe. On May 5, 1949, after seven months of negotiation, the Brussels powers and five other countries initialled the Treaty embodying the Statute of the Council of Europe.

Three months later, the Council of Europe's Consultative Assembly held its first meeting in Strasbourg, electing as its President Paul-Henri Spaak. The watchword of this first session was the British Labour delegate R. W. G. MacKay's demand for "a political authority for Europe with limited functions but real powers".[15] To achieve it, many plans were debated. The rapporteur for the Economic Affairs Committee, Sir (then Mr.) David Eccles, proposed a link between the Council and the O.E.E.C.; a French M.R.P. deputy, Robert Buron, proposed that the O.E.E.C. set about achieving a "European Economic Union"; Mr. MacKay proposed a European Bank. More ambitious still, André Philip and Paul Reynaud demanded the "creation of a political authority of a supranational character". At the end of the session, Spaak declared: "I came to Strasbourg convinced of the necessity of a United States of Europe. I am leaving it with the certitude that union is possible."[16]

Bliss was it in that dawn to be alive. Looking back across the yellowing, dusty archives of barely thirteen years ago, it is hard to write without irony or bitterness of so many disappointed hopes. In 1949, faith—and public pressure—seemed to have moved mountains: an official Assembly of parliamentarians from ten countries had been established: excitement was in the air:

the possibilities seemed boundless. And, indeed, the Council of Europe marked an important advance. It was a distinctly political body which sought to make a break with purely intergovernmental traditions. The members of its Assembly, elected by their national parliaments from among the political parties, took their seats in alphabetical order, not in national delegations, and were able to develop something approaching a European point of view. The *Maison de l'Europe*, specially constructed in Strasbourg in the spring of 1950, provided both a concrete symbol of the new entity and invaluable material facilities, with a debating chamber permanently wired for simultaneous interpretation, a series of recording studios and Press rooms, and well-equipped if spartan offices for delegates and staff. As a broad forum for European discussion, the Council was to perform unspectacular but useful tasks of fact-finding, contact-making, fund-raising and cultural and legal co-ordination. Its most notable achievement was to be the European Convention for the Protection of Human Rights, later backed by a European Court. Its scholarships and studies were to spread mutual knowledge and understanding among its member nations; and it incidentally recruited for its Secretariat a number of remarkably devoted and talented men and women, many of whom were later to be tempted away to the institutions of the European Community.

This drift away from Strasbourg, however, was itself symptomatic of growing dissatisfaction with the achievements of the Council of Europe—a feeling which found its sharpest expression when Paul-Henri Spaak resigned from the Presidency of the Consultative Assembly in December, 1951. By then, it had become clear that the reality of the Strasbourg conclave was a pale shadow of its founders' aspirations, and that the basic reason for this lay outside the control of either its delegates or its Secretariat. What was at fault was the structure of the institution itself.

The original plans submitted by the European Movement had

envisaged a large Assembly of some three or four hundred parliamentary delegates, with a European Council of Ministers playing a relatively minor rôle. During the negotiation of the Statute, France and Belgium had proposed an Assembly similar to that suggested by the European Movement, with a slightly more prominent intergovernmental Council. Great Britain, on the other hand, was unenthusiastic about the idea of a parliamentary Assembly, and had first proposed only a "Council of Europe" formed from government-appointed delegations, later modifying this project to include a Committee of Ministers on the one hand and a Conference of Delegates, again government-appointed, on the other. The final compromise, whose outlines were agreed in January, 1949, provided for a Committee of Ministers, an international Secretariat, and an Assembly practically stripped of any power.[17]

In the early days of the Consultative Assembly, indeed, it was not even permitted to decide its own agenda; and even when it had been granted this right, it could still only submit resolutions to the Committee of Ministers. The latter, in fact, was the "executive" body : unlike the Committee of O.E.E.C., however, it could not take decisions binding upon member governments, but only make recommendations to them. Moreover, although it was formally empowered to decide many questions by majority vote, it nevertheless preferred to seek unanimous agreement, thereby virtually imposing upon itself the possibility of a national veto. This, together with the fact that the Committee too often, in the Assembly's view, met only at official, not at Ministerial level, seemed to reflect a general lack of interest in the Council of Europe which in turn led to bad blood between the Ministers and the Assembly. Attempts to reform the Council's structure met with little success; and by 1957 the Consultative Assembly's Bureau declared its sad conclusion "that the 'Fifteen' [member governments] have no common political will on the questions to which the Assembly devotes most of its time". This was only a polite paraphrase of the bitter judgment delivered years earlier by Paul Reynaud. "The Council of Europe," he said, "consists of two bodies, one of them *for* Europe, and the other *against* it."[18]

The winter of 1949-50, therefore, was a time of mixed feelings on the part of those who hoped for real unity in Europe. The O.E.E.C. and the Council of Europe were undoubtedly important and valuable—more so, indeed, than some champions of a more radical approach were often willing to admit. But there was nevertheless a very deep sense of disquiet and frustration, and much casting about for ways of making a fresh start. The world situation was still grave, and seemed to be worsening; and in Western Europe itself new problems and new dangers were beginning to arise. It was against this darkening background that a new and revolutionary chapter in the story was now to be opened by the Declaration of Monsieur Robert Schuman, French Foreign Minister, on May 9, 1950.

CHAPTER V

FROM THE SCHUMAN PLAN TO THE DEFEAT OF E.D.C.

THE EUROPEAN COMMUNITY was born at four o'clock on a fine spring afternoon in Paris. Invited to the Quai d'Orsay for a Press conference on May 9, 1950, many journalists were inclined to treat it as just another French Foreign Office briefing; but when the time came, about a hundred people crowded into the ornate and gilded Salon de l'Horloge, with its sprawling cherubs and massive chandeliers. Punctually at four, Robert Schuman, French Foreign Minister, entered the room accompanied by his senior officials. Tall, thin, elderly, slightly stooping, with his habitual air of a wise, benevolent, and rather preoccupied professor, he made his way quickly—almost furtively, one observer thought—to the empty place under the chimneypiece clock at the head of a hollow square of green-baize-covered tables. Adjusting a pair of heavy-framed spectacles, he began to read from the paper he carried in his hand. The traditional setting made a sharp contrast with the tone of his opening statement:

"It is no longer the moment for vain words, but for a bold act—a constructive act."

With this, he launched what Walter Lippmann was to call "the most audacious and constructive initiative since the end of the war." For the assembled journalists, the main news story was contained in a paragraph that came later: "The French government proposes to place the whole of Franco-German coal and steel output under a common High Authority, in an organization open to the participation of the other countries of Europe." But the Declaration and its preamble went much further than that. In essence, they were an attempt to tackle both long-term and short-term problems; and because they foreshadowed so much that followed, it is worth examining them in some detail and in the context of their time.[1]

Their first long-term aim was the achievement of European unity as a stabilizing factor in favour of world peace. Since September, 1949, the Soviet Union had publicly acknowledged possession of the atomic bomb; and Western Europe could scarcely afford to remain weak and fragmented, with a potentially explosive area of instability in the form of a divided Germany. "World peace can only be safeguarded by creative efforts which match the dangers that threaten it." "For peace to have a real chance, there must first be a Europe." "The contribution that an organized and living Europe can bring to civilization is indispensable to the maintenance of peaceful relations. . . . Europe was not built, and we had war." The final goal was therefore "the European federation which is indispensable to the maintenance of peace".[2]

But "the gathering together of European nations requires the elimination of the age-old opposition between France and Germany". This had a particular meaning in 1950. In the summer of 1948, the American, British, and French military governors of the three Western zones of Germany had invited the leaders of the eleven Western *Länder*, or provinces, to set up a constituent assembly. A parliamentary council had been formed, with Konrad Adenauer as its president, to prepare a Constitution, known as the Basic Law, which had come into force in May, 1949. Although France, Britain, and the United States still retained control of armaments, foreign affairs, and other matters, it was clear that eventually the German Federal Republic would have to be re-admitted to full status. At the time, for many people in France and elsewhere, this was a more revolutionary step than it seems today, when memories of the Nazis and of World War II are older and fainter by twelve years; and there was then an even more obvious need to prevent the new Republic from playing the tempting rôle of an Eastern European third force. In order to cement the resurgent Germany to the West, "five years almost to the day after Germany's unconditional surrender, France is taking the first decisive step in the construction of Europe, and is associating Germany with it". "The solidarity . . . thus achieved will make it plain that any war between France and Germany becomes not only unthinkable but materially impossible."

To achieve these basic aims, it was necessary both to make a breakthrough on a narrower front and to solve a number of immediate problems. "Europe will not be made all at once, or as a single whole : it will be built by concrete achievements which first create *de facto* solidarity." This was an echo of the "functionalism" which had already been proposed in the Council of Europe, especially by British spokesmen, as an alternative to the somewhat bull-headed federalism of those who wished to set up European political institutions without assigning them specific and concrete tasks. Coal and steel, the munitions of war and the basis of heavy industry, were a promising point of departure for the functionalist method. Geology is no respecter of nations; and since 1870, at least, both France and Germany had been aware that Europe's biggest concentration of coal and iron ore, and hence of steel production, lay within a comparatively small area —the Ruhr, Lorraine, parts of northern France, the Saar, Luxembourg, most of Belgium, and part of the Netherlands— whose natural unity was criss-crossed by national frontiers. Lord Keynes was only one of many to point out the economic advantages to be gained from integrating what was essentially an interdependent complex of resources.[3]

This, however, at once posed the problem of how to control such an integrated area of production, otherwise than through its seizure by one of the larger European powers. In 1926, an international cartel had been formed by Belgian, French, Luxembourg, and Saarland steel producers; but although hailed by some as "an experiment in international co-operation", this had both proved ineffective and aroused the not unnatural suspicions of those who felt, like the American expert C. K. Leith, that the area was "the arsenal of Europe, which should not be left to commercial control".[4] Such reasoning was greatly strengthened by the two world wars. Ever since its occupation by France in 1923, the Ruhr had been a bone of contention; and before the end of World War II General de Gaulle had called for its severance from Germany. In 1947, France proposed a system of international control and Allied ownership of German coal and steel, and although in its initial form this was not accepted by Great Britain and the United States, it eventually led to an Agreement, signed in April 1949, setting up the International Authority for the Ruhr, in which Germany had a minority voice. The Authority, however, was weak, and triply unpopular— with France, who wanted to strengthen it, with Great Britain and the United States, who doubted whether it was necessary, and with Germany, who disliked such unilateral application of control. The Schuman Plan pointed to a way out of all these difficulties, by extending control to French and other heavy industry and at the same time diluting the forces of nationalism in a wider European pool. "The pooling of coal and steel production will immediately provide for the establishment of common bases for economic development as a first step in the federation of Europe, and will change the destinies of those regions which have long been devoted to the manufacture of munitions of war, of which they have been the most constant victims."

A parallel but dissimilar problem was that of the Saar. Unlike the Ruhr, this had been formally attached to France since 1947. From April 1949, Saar coal production had gradually been transferred to France; but the negotiation of the Franco-Saar

Conventions during that year, confirming that the Saar was politically autonomous but economically French, caused serious tension with the new German government. Here again the Schuman Plan seemed to promise an amicable solution—and in fact it was to facilitate the cooling-off of the Saar problem when after the 1955 elections, which showed an overwhelming majority in favour of links with Germany, France agreed to return the territory to the Federal Republic in June 1956.

One further short-term problem also made its contribution to the Schuman Plan. The slight United States recession of 1949, coupled with the rapid expansion of European steel capacity, had led to a slackening in the market and a quickening of fears that manufacturers were preparing to re-establish price rings. In December, the Economic Commission for Europe had published an influential report calling for measures to increase steel consumption, to co-ordinate investment programmes and supplies of raw materials, and to develop productivity : cartels, it pointed out, were a purely negative, restrictive, and short-sighted remedy. As it turned out, the danger of over-production in steel proved illusory : but it gave further stimulus to the Schuman proposals : "In contrast to international cartels, which seek to divide and exploit international markets by restrictive practices and the maintenance of high profits, the proposed organization will ensure the fusion of markets and the expansion of production."

The Declaration concluded by calling for institutions of a type radically different from those established either in the O.E.E.C. or in the Council of Europe. "The common High Authority entrusted with the working of the whole system will be composed of independent persons designated by governments on a basis of parity. . . . Its decisions will have the force of law in France, in Germany, and in the other member countries. Appropriate provisions will ensure the necessary means of appeal."

Nor, finally, was the process to stop there. The Declaration looked ahead to something very like the future Common

Market. "This transformation will make possible other joint actions which have been impossible until now." "Thus will be realized, simply and rapidly, the fusion of interests which is indispensable to the establishment of an economic community; thus will be introduced the germ of a broader and deeper community between countries long opposed to one another by bloody conflicts." It added: "Europe will be able, with increased resources, to pursue the realization of one of her essential tasks, the development of the African continent."

Such, then, was the project that Robert Schuman announced to the world on May 9, 1950. Although it bears his name, it has long been an open secret that the initiative behind it was that of Jean Monnet, then in charge of the French Reconstruction Plan —"*le Plan*". The Declaration itself was evidently a collaborative effort: the preamble is said to have been written by Jacques Gascuel, editor of the magazine *Perspectives*; the economic sections are attributed to Pierre Uri, then one of Monnet's assistants on the *Plan*; the institutional passage is said to have been composed by Paul Reuter, Professor of Law at Aix; and the allusion to African development is ascribed to René Mayer, later to succeed Monnet as President of the High Authority.[5] But the very words—"indispensable", "essential", "rapid", "concrete", "immediate"—bear Monnet's distinctive stamp.

Most of the separate ideas in the proposal, again, were common currency at the time: but it was Monnet who saw their interdependence and made of them a constructive and dynamic plan, and it was he who set about the still more difficult task of getting the plan accepted. His patience, his alertness, his untiring insistence, his curious inspired impulsiveness, his sense of timing, and above all his realization that projects are furthered not just by advocacy but by creating conditions that ensure their fulfilment—all these help to explain the very great prestige and influence that he has enjoyed in postwar Europe. But there is also a more personal aspect. Short, sturdy, energetic, and down-to-earth, with perpetually raised eyebrows and a quiet, quick voice, Monnet somewhat resembles the French comedian Noël-Noël; but he has a warmth, a twinkling geniality, and a very genuine kindness that are extraordinarily difficult to resist. He has always been able to inspire devotion among the small and effective multi-national teams with whom he works; and the same qualities have ensured him a sympathetic hearing when putting forward his ideas elsewhere. It was thus not long after Monnet had first communicated the elements of the later Declaration to Bernard Clappier, then Robert Schuman's *chef de cabinet*, that Schuman decided to present the project to his colleagues in the French government. To Schuman as well as Monnet, therefore, must go the credit of having seen it through.

The response to the Schuman Declaration was immediate. By the end of May, Belgium, Germany, Italy, Luxembourg, and the Netherlands had all agreed to consider the proposals; and although the Netherlands government had some reservations of principle about the "supranational" High Authority, negotiations were quickly under way. That they were not easy was to be expected, for there was considerable opposition to so unprecedented a step. Nevertheless, Schuman may not have been entirely mistaken when, looking back afterwards, he said: "The six delegations were in some sense allies, pooling their knowledge and their goodwill."[6] At least four of the leaders of the countries in question were especially sympathetic to the project because they came from regions which had been the victims of successive wars. Schuman himself had been brought up in Alsace under German domination, and educated at a German school. Adenauer, Chancellor of the new German Republic, was a Rhinelander who as long ago as the 1920's had declared that "a lasting peace between France and Germany can only be attained through the establishment of a community of economic interests between the two countries".[7] Alcide de Gasperi, the Italian Prime Minister, came from the Trentino, which had been under Austrian rule until 1918. Thus all three could incidentally converse in fluent German. A fourth important figure was the Belgian Socialist Paul-Henri Spaak, whose country had been invaded in two world wars, as had Luxembourg; while the Netherlands had similarly been overrun in World War II.

Under this leadership, and with a negotiating committee which included Jean Monnet and Walter Hallstein, the Treaty establishing the European Coal and Steel Community was drawn up within a year; signed on April 18, 1951, it was ratified by the summer of 1952. In contrast to the original Schuman proposals, it provided for a Common Assembly and a Council of Ministers as well as a High Authority and a Court; but its Preamble was practically a digest of the Schuman Declaration, including many of the same words and phrases. To implement it, the member states' Foreign Ministers met in Paris on July 23-25, 1952 : on the principle that "the devil is in the details", what should have been a merely formal occasion developed into a debate about the Community's official languages and the site of its headquarters. France proposed respectively French and Saarbrücken; but after long discussion, French, German, Italian, and Dutch became the Community languages, Strasbourg the seat of the Common Assembly, and Luxembourg that of the High Authority and the Court of Justice. The latter decision, indeed, was not even "provisional", as is usually suggested : to avoid a late-night deadlock, the Ministers merely agreed to hold their next meeting in Luxembourg.[8] Appointing the High Authority proved somewhat easier. Monnet became its first President, with Franz Etzel, later German Finance Minister, and Albert Coppé, former Belgian Economic Affairs Minister, as its two Vice-Presidents, although the Treaty only called for one. The other members were Dirk Spierenburg, head of the Dutch delegation to the O.E.E.C. and to the Schuman Treaty conference; Albert Wehrer, who had headed the Luxembourg delegation in the negotiations; Enzo Giacchero, a Vice-President of the Italian parliamentary

Christian-Democrat party and an active federalist; Léon Daum, a French industrialist and coal-steel expert; and Heinz Potthoff, a former German steelworker who had been a member of the International Authority for the Ruhr. These eight members then co-opted a ninth, the Belgian Paul Finet, first president of the International Confederation of Free Trade Unions. So constituted, the High Authority held its first meeting in Luxembourg on August 10, 1952.[9]

In considering the achievements of the European Coal and Steel Community, it is convenient to distinguish, rather as does the E.C.S.C. Treaty, between three aspects of its work—the "fusion of markets" by the removal of barriers to intra-Community trade in coal and steel; the expansion of the economy and the improvement of living standards by means of concerted policies; and the preparation of further steps towards unity.

The removal of trade barriers—customs duties, quantitative restrictions, dual pricing, currency restrictions, and transport discrimination—was rapidly set in motion. The "common market" for coal, iron ore, and scrap was opened on February 10, 1953; that for steel on May 1, 1953; and that for "special steels"[10] on August 1, 1954. By 1958, when the Community's five-year transition period ended and national tariffs on imports from non-member countries were harmonized, intra-Community trade in coal had increased by 21 per cent, in coke by 14.8 per cent, in iron ore by 25.5 per cent, in scrap by 175 per cent, and in steel by 157 per cent.

The difficulties of adapting to this new situation had been stressed by both Left and Right during the ratification debates in the national parliaments; but experience had shown that adjustment could be comparatively easy in a period of rapid economic growth. In some respects, moreover, it had been especially eased. During the transition period, Italy had been allowed to taper off her duties on coke and steel imports from her Community partners, and other transitional aid had been given to French, Belgian, and Sardinian coal. What was more, the makers of the Treaty had taken steps to ensure that the brunt of economic change was not borne by labour in the form of technological unemployment, as for example during the Industrial Revolution; and sizeable funds were made available for the retraining and resettlement of those who lost or changed their jobs. By the end of the transition period, in fact, the total number employed in the Community's coal and steel industries was 80,000 greater than in 1952, and gross hourly earnings had increased by about 21 per cent; but the equivalent of $4.5 million had been spent in grants for 20,000 displaced workers. At the same time, some $60 million was allocated for the building of 38,000 new houses and flats. With one major exception, in fact, the transition to a single market in coal and steel was achieved fairly smoothly.

The Coal and Steel Community saw the light in a period of general expansion which undoubtedly helped to account for its economic success. During its first five years, coke production rose by 23.7 per cent to 77.2 million metric tons, iron ore production by 33.8 per cent to 87.4 million, and pig iron production by 29.6 per cent to 45 million. Even more spectacular was the expansion in steel. Here, output rose by 42 per cent, to reach 59.8 million metric tons in 1957 : by 1960, it stood at 73 million, or 21.3 per cent of total world production, as against 19.8 per cent in 1952. Steel prices meanwhile rose by only 3 per cent between 1953 and 1960, as compared with much more rapid increases in Great Britain and the United States. Much of this progress was due to the high and steady level of investments, which rose from $545 million in the steel industry in 1952 to an estimated $838 million in 1960, only seriously dipping during the slight recession of 1954. During this whole period, the High Authority itself provided loans totalling $421 million to coal and steel investment projects involving $1,300 million; and it spent an additional $16 million on technical research.

The one exception to this encouraging picture was the problem of coal. Even during the five-year transition period, coal production expanded less rapidly than that of other industries, increasing by only 3.8 per cent to 247.8 million metric tons in 1957. In the following year, when a further slight recession struck Europe, deep-seated changes in the pattern of energy consumption suddenly became glaringly apparent: coal was losing the battle against oil. Total energy needs were still increasing, but much more rapidly than coal consumption. Whereas in 1950 coal had provided 80 per cent of the Community's energy supplies, in 1958 it provided only 64.5 per cent; and by 1960 this figure had dropped to 59.5 per cent. Meanwhile, the proportion supplied by oil, methane, and natural gas rose from 13.1 per cent in 1950 to 27.4 per cent in 1958 and 32.3 per cent in 1960. Coupled with a series of mild winters, this spelt crisis for the Community's higher-cost coalmines, particularly in the Belgian Borinage; short-time working began, and pithead stocks rose to a record total of 31 million metric tons in 1959. The High Authority asked the member states to sanction the use of its emergency powers to regulate Community imports: failing this, the governments themselves reduced their imports from outside the Community, which fell from 43.9 million metric tons in 1957 to 17.8 in 1960. Meanwhile, the High Authority temporarily isolated the Belgian coal market, and made resettlement grants totalling some $30 million to 95,000 miners. Ironically enough, the recipients of High Authority aid tended to blame their troubles on the Community rather than on the long-term decline in the relative position of coal; and in 1961 I myself saw Borinage miners carrying angry placards condemning the very organization that was easing their inevitably unhappy lot.

The problem of coal also affected the E.C.S.C.'s record in dealing with mergers and cartels. Although it has no mandate to expropriate or nationalize coal or steel firms, the High Authority has a particular duty to prevent monopolies and price-rings.

Mergers between firms are subject to its prior authorization, but are generally regarded as "innocent" unless they are proved "guilty". The High Authority has stated, however, that it would not authorize the formation of a group as large and as powerful as the old *Vereinigte Stahlwerke*, which before the war produced nearly 40 per cent of Germany's steel; and independent studies have tended to confirm that even in industries too prone to large concentrations, and even in the Community-scale market, this situation has not in fact been reached.[11] Cartels, on the other hand, are regarded much more severely by the E.C.S.C. Treaty. In times of glut or shortage, the Community itself has residual power to impose production quotas or maximum prices and allocation of scarce supplies; but in normal times its task is to ensure free competition by enforcing publication of prices and non-discrimination between customers, as well as by preventing price-rigging and other concerted practices between firms. Here, it has enjoyed a number of early successes, but has sometimes been handicapped by the difficulty of proof; and the special problems of the coal industry have increased the complications involved in tackling both the German coal-exporting organiza- tions and their French coal-importing counterpart. Despite the abolition of the German *Gemeinschaftsorganisation Ruhrkohle* (GEORG) and the modification of the French *Association Tech- nique de l'Importation Charbonnière* (A.T.I.C.), pressure for some relaxation of the rules in this sphere remains strong, although a recent decision of the Court of Justice, in December, 1961, implied that this would require full-scale amendment of the Schuman Treaty.

If in this way the achievements of the E.C.S.C. still remain incomplete, a third aspect of its activities was to be still more important to the future development of Europe: that is, their institutional framework. In the Preamble to the Treaty, the member states spoke of their intention "to lay the bases of institutions capable of giving direction to their common destiny";

and Monnet, in particular, declared that "I was long ago struck by a reflection made by the Swiss philosopher Amiel, who said : 'Each man's experience starts again from the beginning. Only institutions grow wiser; they accumulate collective experience, and owing to this experience and this wisdom, men subject to the same rules will not see their own nature changing, but their behaviour gradually transformed.' "[12]

In fact, the institutions of the E.C.S.C. differed in several significant respects from those of a traditional international organization. Even its Council of Ministers, whose members were national representatives, was subject in many cases to majority voting : as Adenauer told the Common Assembly on the second day of its first session in September, 1952, "The Council of Ministers is not a Ministerial Council such as we know them in the conferences of international organizations. It is an element organically included in the new supranational European Community."[13] The Common Assembly, although far from being a Parliament, had the substantial power of ousting the High Authority, which with the Court of Justice was the most clearly "supranational" of the Community's institutions, although much debate ensued as to what this adjective meant.[14] The High Authority, in particular, was not composed of national representatives but of independent members forbidden to solicit or take instructions, and deciding by simple majority vote which then involved collective responsibility even for the minority, as in a national Cabinet. In many cases, the High Authority could act without obtaining the prior approval of member governments—a power which it was careful, perhaps too careful, not to abuse. Community decisions were directly binding in the territories of the member states, without having to be embodied in national legislation. The High Authority levied its own tax on coal and steel production, and its tax and price inspectors had direct access to company books. It was responsible to the Common Assembly, not to the national parliaments, and the only appeal from its valid decisions was to the Court of Justice, whose verdicts were final and binding on persons, firms, institutions, and governments.

Such elaborate institutions were clearly intended to have an importance outside the field of coal and steel: the first General Report of the High Authority, indeed, submitted to the Common Assembly on April 11, 1953, was significantly entitled *The Activities of the European Community*, with the words "coal and steel" quietly omitted. "The European Coal and Steel Community," said Monnet, "is the first expression of the Europe that is being born."[15] The High Authority's Information Service, while effectively publicizing news of coal and steel developments and of the High Authority's specific activities, also developed into a kind of semi-official information centre spreading "the European idea" in general; and in the minds of all those who followed Monnet to Luxembourg—including many from rue Martignac, the Paris headquarters of the French *Plan*—the European Coal and Steel Community, although important in itself, was chiefly a pilot plant preparing for further ventures.

Already, indeed, the Schuman Declaration had stimulated a number of short-lived projects for integration in other sectors, for the most part closely modelled on the E.C.S.C. Of these, the most noteworthy were the proposals for a European Agricultural Community (the so-called "Green Pool"), for a European Transport Authority, and for a European Health Community (the "White Pool").

A European organization of markets for a number of agricultural products was first mooted in the early summer of 1950, both by the Committee of the O.E.E.C. and by Monsieur Pierre Pflimlin, who in June submitted a draft Resolution on the subject to the French National Assembly. In August, the Consultative Assembly of the Council of Europe recommended that a conference be held to study the idea; and in November Mr. S. L. Mansholt, then Dutch Minister of Agriculture and now a

Vice-President of the Common Market Commission, proposed what amounted to a full "common market" in agriculture under a supranational Authority. The Consultative Assembly subsequently approved a report calling for institutions similar to those of the E.C.S.C., with a wide range of powers to balance production and consumption, fix prices, and set up a single market; but meanwhile Pflimlin himself, now Minister of Agriculture, had persuaded the French Government to propose to its O.E.E.C. partners a European Agricultural Community, with institutions based on the Coal and Steel Community pattern, to bring about a gradual integration of European agricultural markets product by product. A preparatory conference met in Paris in March, 1952; but in the face of opposition from the farming lobbies, the original proposals had been considerably watered down. Even so, the British, Swedish, and Norwegian governments felt unable to consider full membership of the proposed organization, and after a European Conference on the subject a year later, the whole project gradually died out in an interim committee whose work was overtaken by later events.

The question of a European transport plan was first raised in August 1950, again in the Consultative Assembly, by Monsieur Edouard Bonnefous, a French Deputy of the Socialist-Republican Union (U.D.S.R.), who proposed a High Authority to run a "European Transport Organization" similar to the E.C.S.C. A special Committee reported on the subject in April 1951, but its suggestions ran into German and Scandinavian opposition. After a counter-proposal from Mr. van de Kieft, of the Netherlands, a third and even less "supranational" project was adopted by the Consultative Assembly, but led to nothing. Finally, on December 31, 1953, it was in the framework of the O.E.E.C. that a purely co-operative European Conference of Transport Ministers was established, with which the E.C.S.C. retained formal and technical links.

The third abortive project was that of a European Health Community, proposed by the French Government in September 1952 on the initiative of its Minister of Health, Monsieur Paul Ribeyre. Its aim was to co-ordinate and improve health protection and hospital facilities in the member states. A draft Treaty to this end, embodying a supranational High Authority and other institutions modelled on those of the E.C.S.C., was submitted to the member governments of the O.E.E.C.; and in December, 1952 a conference met in Paris, with representatives from the Community countries, Great Britain, Switzerland, and Turkey. Save, however, for a final resolution calling upon governments to appoint experts to study the French draft, this proposal thereafter sank without trace.[16]

Amid these various plans for further "sector integration", however, two major projects stood out. The first was the European Defence Community, the second the European Political Community. A great deal of political and emotional capital was invested in both of them, and the chart of their changing fortunes is an important element in the present story.

The outbreak of the Korean War in July 25, 1950, redoubled the apprehension which had been building up during the past years of "cold war". "Western Europe," in the words of one fairly detached observer, "half expected a repetition of the Korean invasion 'by proxy' in the following year."[17] What was more, the crisis found the Atlantic allies very much underprepared. N.A.T.O. possessed fourteen scattered divisions and 1,000 aircraft, as compared with 175 Soviet divisions and 20,000 Soviet planes. With France deeply committed to the war in Indo-China, the United States began seriously to re-examine the defence position in Europe. On August 30, Germany asked for more Allied troops to be stationed in her territory, as well as for permission to raise an armed mobile police force as a counter to the similar *"Bereitschaften"* in the Soviet zone. On September 9, President Truman promised more U.S. troops, and on September 26 the N.A.T.O. Council agreed to set up an integrated command. But on September 12, Dean Acheson, the Secretary of State, had already gone one step further and proposed to his British and French colleagues that German divisions should be raised to serve under N.A.T.O.

Five years after the end of World War II, this suggestion came as a shock. The prospect of a re-armed Germany, at that time not yet anchored to the West even by the Coal and Steel Community, was enough to make many Europeans react with "I don't know if they'd frighten the Russians, but by God they'd frighten me". It was at this point that there came the sudden brainwave—why not create a multinational army, in which German contingents would be under European command? Thus the defence problem would be solved without reviving the *Wehrmacht*, and a huge stride would be taken in the direction of federal unity in Europe.

The basic idea of a European army had already been proposed in the Consultative Assembly of the Council of Europe by André Philip, the French Socialist, and a few days later, on August 11, 1950, in a motion by Winston Churchill. These proposals, however, were somewhat vague. A slightly more concrete project was suggested on October 8 by Arthur Koestler, in an article in *The New York Times*: this envisaged a kind of European Foreign Legion in which each platoon would comprise soldiers of different nationalities.[18] But the decisive plan was that presented to the French National Assembly on October 24 by Prime Minister René Pleven, and approved by 343 votes to 225. After some discussions with N.A.T.O. representatives, this led to the convening of a Treaty-making conference and eventually to the signature by the six E.C.S.C. countries of the European Defence Community (E.D.C.) Treaty on May 27, 1952. This ceremony, like the original Schuman Declaration, took place in the Salon de l'Horloge at the Quai d'Orsay.

The E.D.C. Treaty provided for institutions closely modelled on those of the Coal and Steel Community—a nine-man executive Commissariat, corresponding to the High Authority; a Council of Ministers, again with majority voting on a number of issues; a Court, to be shared with the E.C.S.C.; and an Assembly which would in fact be the E.C.S.C.'s Common Assembly slightly enlarged. As a general rule, national armed forces would be replaced by a European Army of some forty divisions—the division to be the smallest national unit, but all to wear a European uniform. The military aspects of the Treaty had been worked out in full liaison with N.A.T.O., and the whole project was endorsed by the United States; moreover, although Great Britain had caused much disappointment by her unwillingness to join the organization, she had nevertheless signed a treaty of mutual assistance with its members on the same day as the E.D.C. Treaty itself. That summer, with the E.C.S.C.'s High Authority established in Luxembourg and E.D.C. awaiting ratification, the barometer appeared to be set fair for rapid European integration.

This prospect seemed to be confirmed, in particular, by Article 38 of the E.D.C. Treaty, which called for further steps towards political federation to be prepared by the E.D.C. Assembly. On September 10, 1952, without waiting for this to be formally constituted, the Council of Ministers of the E.C.S.C. asked the members of its nascent Common Assembly to co-opt further members into a so-called "Ad hoc Assembly" in order to draft the Treaty for a European Political Community (E.P.C.) as soon as possible. Meeting for the first time on September 15, the Ad hoc Assembly finally approved a draft Treaty on March 10, 1953. This provided for a European Executive Council, to be entitled "Ministers of the European Community"; a Council of national Ministers; a Court; and a Parliament, comprising a Senate appointed by the national parliaments and a Peoples' Chamber directly elected on a Community basis. Within two years the E.C.S.C. and E.D.C. institutions were intended to be fused into those of the E.P.C., without, however, abrogating their respective powers.

Even before the Ad hoc Assembly had held its first meeting, some voices had expressed scepticism about such a plan. Speaking in the E.C.S.C.'s Common Assembly, Monsieur Michel Debré, subsequently French Prime Minister, had declared that he was "favourable to a European political authority . . . but . . . this political authority must have a confederal character".[19] Later he added : "We have never worked in a satisfactory way to find out what this authority would be, what would be its tasks, and what would be the political system of Europe. There is a silence that has gone on for a long time, which shows that we have before us very different and very divergent ideas."[20] Although the final draft Treaty was adopted by 50 to 0, many members of the Ad hoc Assembly abstained or stayed away from the vote. If the Assembly was divided, moreover, the Ministers were lukewarm about its proposals. Georges Bidault, in particular, spoke ominously of the "inevitable division of labour between men with bold and independent minds and governments whose honour and impediment it is to carry the responsibility".[21] Meeting successively in the summer and autumn of 1953, in Paris, Baden-Baden, and The Hague, the Foreign Ministers appointed a committee of officials to work out fresh proposals; but while these were being debated the prospects of the European Political Community were already darkening as the storm-clouds began to gather about its parent project, E.D.C.

The first national parliament to vote on the E.D.C. Treaty was the German *Bundestag*. The Social Democrats, who had voted against the E.C.S.C., were also opposed to E.D.C., partly because they feared that it might prejudice the eventual reunification of Germany; but there were certainly tactical elements in their opposition, and it did not prevent a substantial majority approving the Treaty on March 19, 1953. Favourable votes quickly followed in the Netherlands, Belgium, and Luxembourg;

and by the spring of 1954 only Italy and France had still not voted. Italy was undergoing a series of Cabinet crises, and tended to wait upon France; but in both countries opposition to E.D.C. was growing. It was based on a number of fairly reasonable arguments—that East-West tension was slackening, particularly since Stalin's death; that for the time being N.A.T.O. afforded adequate defence; that it would be a mistake to drive too ruthlessly towards federation and risk ructions later; that the E.D.C. formula would divide the French army; that the absence of Great Britain from the future organization would give too great a weight to Germany. Such doubts as these were serious enough to be shared by men of several political parties, from Gaullists to French and even Italian (Nenni) Socialists. They were tirelessly exploited, however, by the extreme right-wing, including in Italy the neo-Fascists and a section of the Monarchists, and in France such prominent figures as Marshal Juin and the Comte de Paris. More aggressive still were the tactics of the Communist party and its sympathizers. In Italy at the time, I was sufficiently struck to report on the extraordinary variety of the methods used—a virulent poster campaign, a series of strikes, shameless exploitation of the Montesi scandal, and even, it seemed, the founding of an extreme left-wing intellectual weekly to compete with the *New Statesman*-like *Il Mondo*, which had consistently supported E.D.C. "German re-armament" was the constant reproach levelled at the plan for a European army, by the left as well as by the right.[22]

But it was in Paris, not Rome, that the final drama was to be played out. When in June 1954 Pierre Mendès-France became Prime Minister at the head of a Gaullist-Radical coalition, it required no great foresight on my part to prophesy that his investiture would be "fatal to French ratification of E.D.C.";[23] and when the Geneva talks on a cease-fire in Indo-China coincided with the fall of the French garrison at Dien Bien Phu, fear turned into virtual certainty. "It was obvious," wrote Raymond

Aron, "that M. Molotov had granted M. Mendès-France the benefit of an armistice—naturally popular in France—in the hope that the French chief of government would reject E.D.C. This was indeed what happened."[24] True, on August 19 Mendès-France made a last-minute bid to have the E.D.C. Treaty amended in a form more acceptable to his government; but when these proposals were rejected by his European colleagues, it was only a matter of time before the blow fell. On August 28, the Prime Minister opened the debate in the French Assembly with a deliberately neutral statement, to be followed by a series of onslaughts from the opposition to E.D.C., of which the most emotional came from Edouard Herriot, once the champion of European unity. On August 30, the Treaty was rejected by 319 votes to 264, with 43 abstentions. The triumphant opposition sang the *Marseillaise*; but elsewhere all was confusion, anger, and dismay.

Within a few weeks—largely thanks to the initiative of the then Mr. Anthony Eden, British Foreign Secretary—another kind of agreement had been patched up to enable Germany to make her contribution to European defence and enjoy full sovereignty again. This was Western European Union, institutionally a pale shadow of E.D.C., with a much less powerful Assembly and no serious pooling of sovereignty. Here, Germany and Italy joined the original Brussels Treaty powers, making seven in all—the United Kingdom and the six European Community countries—and Great Britain agreed not to withdraw from the continent her four divisions and tactical air force against the wishes of a majority of the signatory states. The military situation had been saved without that "agonizing reappraisal" of United States policies that John Foster Dulles had threatened in December, 1953.[25] The new arrangements limited Germany's contribution to 12 divisions, and imposed on her a unilateral undertaking not to manufacture large-scale weapons: but it was ironical, to say the least, that those who had opposed E.D.C. because it meant

"German re-armament" within a European defence force now found themselves faced with a German army in the looser framework of W.E.U.

Moreover, when E.D.C. failed, the European Political Community failed with it. Almost simultaneously, the streets of Rome were filled with crowds making their last tribute to the funeral procession of Alcide de Gasperi, the greatest of the Italian "Europeans". Two months later, when Jean Monnet announced that he would not seek re-election as President of the E.C.S.C. High Authority, it looked as if the postwar movement towards unity in Europe was coming to an end.

CHAPTER VI

FROM MESSINA TO BRUSSELS—EURATOM AND THE COMMON MARKET

THE DEFEAT OF E.D.C. marked the end of one avenue of approach to European unity : but it also made clear how resilient and resourceful the integration movement was. Announcing his decision to leave the High Authority, Jean Monnet stressed that it was "in order to be able to take part with complete freedom of action and speech in the construction of European unity";[1] and he was not the only European to look ahead. On December 2, 1954, the E.C.S.C.'s Common Assembly called for the establishment of a working group to study possible extensions of the Community's purview. By this means it was in fact to keep a close watch on future developments; and on May 14, 1955, it proposed not only wider application of the E.C.S.C., but also the convening of an intergovernmental conference to prepare further steps in European integration. These requests were explicitly directed at the Conference of Foreign Ministers which met in Messina on June 1 and 2. Although its first task was to appoint a successor to Jean Monnet, it also had before it three governmental memoranda on the subject of further integration. The first, of May 20, was from the Benelux countries, whose governments believed that "the moment has come to pass to a new stage in European integration" and that "this must be achieved first in the economic field". The second, from Germany, was drafted in more flexible terms, but called in particular for the founding of a European university; the third, from Italy, laid

especial stress on the social and economic development aspects
of future plans.

The President at the Messina meeting was the jovial, mous-
tachioed, rather Chestertonian Joseph Bech, Prime Minister,
Foreign Minister, and Wine Minister of Luxembourg : the other
countries were represented by Monsieur Spaak, for Belgium; by
Antoine Pinay, for France; by Gaetano Martino, for Italy; by
Johan Willem Beyen, for the Netherlands; and by Walter Hallstein, for Germany. On the first day, in restricted session, they
chose the former French Prime Minister, René Mayer, to succeed
Monnet on the High Authority; then they turned to the discussion of broader questions and the drafting of a final Resolution.
The resultant text was a patchwork of all three governmental
memoranda : but to study the achievement of its various aims it
set up a committee of national representatives, assisted by experts
from the High Authority and other bodies, under the presidency
of Paul-Henri Spaak.

The significance of this decision was threefold. First, although
the final communiqué concealed, like all good communiqués,
some contrasts of opinion, there was a fundamental political con-
sensus on the aims to be achieved. The experts' task was to study
methods, not to debate principles. Secondly, the chairmanship of
Spaak, personally and politically imposing, was to ensure coher-
ence and drive throughout the lengthy meetings that followed.
Thirdly, the presence of High Authority participants—chief
among them Dirk Spierenburg and Pierre Uri, now head of its
Economics Division—meant that continuity with the existing
European Community institutions was carried right down into
the detailed drafting of the new proposals, which drew quite
heavily on the experience already acquired.

The Committee held its first meeting on Saturday, July 9,
1955, at the Ministry of Foreign Affairs in Brussels. Thereafter,
it was to meet in the Château de Val Duchesse, in a wooded park
on the outskirts of the city. Here, with periodic interruptions for

further directives from the Ministers, it hammered out its conclusions, which Spaak presented on March 13, 1956, to a special meeting of the Common Assembly in the Belgian Senate chamber; they were then handed to the Ministers in their final form on April 21, 1956. Meeting in Venice on May 29, the Ministers adopted the Spaak Report,[2] as it came to be called, and virtually transformed the Spaak Committee into a Treaty-making conference, which held its first meeting on June 26.[3] Within a year, the conference had produced the Treaties establishing a European Atomic Energy Community (Euratom) and a European Economic Community (the general Common Market), which were signed on March 25, 1957, in the grand Sala degli Orazi e Curiazi, on the Capitoline Hill in Rome. Ratified by mid-December, they came into force on January 1, 1958 : simultaneously, a special set of protocols provided for a single Assembly and Court, common to the three Community organizations, to replace those of the E.C.S.C. On January 6 and 7, the Foreign Ministers of the Community countries met in Paris to appoint the members of the new bodies' Executives : failing to agree on a joint location for the three Community organizations, they compromised by suggesting that the two new Executives should meet in both Luxembourg and Brussels. Within a few months, the latter had become the provisional *de facto* headquarters of Euratom and the Common Market.

Despite their impressive speed, the negotiations had not been without difficulty; and the whole process would undoubtedly have gone less smoothly without the efforts of Jean Monnet. Within a week of handing over to René Mayer on June 10, 1955, he had entered the campaign for further unity with a widely publicized article in *The Times*,[4] but for some while afterwards it was not clear how best he could use his new-found freedom. Some said that he regretted it, and one of his close advisers even suggested that he should stand for the French National Assembly. Monnet, however, decided otherwise. On October 14, 1955, he

announced the formation of a completely new organization—the
Action Committee for the United States of Europe.

The Action Committee was—and is—no gathering of academic political theorists or fanatical federalists, but a solid and
sober group of thirty-three leading representatives of all shades of
authoritative political and trade-union opinion, except the extreme right and the Communists. In addition to many party
leaders already known for their support of European unity, its
founder-members included the German Socialist Erich Ollen-
hauer, whose party had opposed the E.C.S.C. and E.D.C.
Treaties—but who were to vote for Euratom and the Common
Market, as well as Maurice Faure, from Mendès-France's Radical
Party, and the French Socialist Guy Mollet, whose party had
been deeply split over E.D.C. It was almost as if, in Great
Britain, Monnet had been able to recruit Hugh Gaitskell, Iain
Macleod, and Jo Grimond, together with George Woodcock and
Frank Cousins. During the months that followed, the Action
Committee was to hold meetings roughly twice a year : each
meeting would debate, amend, and vote a draft resolution pains-
takingly prepared by Monnet and his small staff—often including
Community officials or ex-officials recruited for the occasion—in
his Avenue Foch flat overlooking the Bois de Boulogne. Once
voted, a resolution would be binding on the members of the
Committee, and in many cases on their parties and trade unions
too. By prodding governments and winning over parliamentary
and trade union opinion, there can be no doubt at all that
Monnet and the Action Committee played a decisive part in
securing the adoption and ratification of the Euratom and
Common Market Treaties.

For the time being, Euratom was Monnet's chief concern—so
much so that the Italian federalist Altiero Spinelli complained
that "this committee, in spite of its ambitious name, is concerned
only with the rapid promotion of an atomic pool."[5] That was
natural enough, however, since in some ways an atomic pool

seemed logically the next step after the coal and steel pool. So long as the scope of integration was limited to coal and steel, problems were bound to arise at those points where European policies in this sector came into friction with national policies for other products and other forms of energy. In so far as this was an incentive for extending the scope of integration, it was one of the first examples of the way in which the movement towards unity progressed by getting into ,difficulties. Several such difficulties indeed occurred during the E.C.S.C.'s transition period. Government control of steel prices, for instance, was forbidden by the E.C.S.C. Treaty; but for some years the French Government continued to control the prices of finished products, which reflected back upon those of crude steel. In coal, a somewhat similar problem arose early in 1956, when the High Authority contemplated removing the price ceiling that it had imposed on coal from the Ruhr, but was warned by the German Government that this would affect the whole range of the economy, for which the Federal Republic, not the E.C.S.C., was responsible. In the end, this difference was settled amicably : but the problem of principle remained. In fact, neither the early shortage nor the later glut of coal could satisfactorily be dealt with on a Community basis if other forms of energy—some of them much more adaptable to varying demand—were to remain subject to purely national control. Atomic energy was a case in point.

As Spaak put it, "the atom and automation are the future."[6] Already the foundation of the European Nuclear Research Council (C.E.R.N.) in 1952, of the European Atomic Energy Society in 1953, and of the International Atomic Energy Agency in 1954 had been a recognition that nuclear energy called for resources of knowledge, research, skill, capital, and supplies on a more than national scale. The need to guarantee the safety of nuclear installations, to protect the health of technicians and of the general public, and to ensure that fissile material was not diverted to unauthorized uses, also pointed in the direction of international action; while the fact that Europe was only just beginning to develop peaceful atomic energy led many "Europeans" to hope—in some degree mistakenly—that an atomic energy Community would have fewer national vested interests to appease. What was more, the prospect of "taming the atom" had caught the imagination. By the spring of 1955 there was widespread discussion of an atomic "pool",[7] and the idea was given further currency both by the controversy about the nature of a future German atomic energy programme and by the Geneva Conference in the summer.

In January 1956, the first meeting of the Action Committee called for a rapid start to be made on the Euratom proposal; and on September 20, pointing to the looming Suez crisis and the likely effect on oil supplies, it suggested the appointment of "Three Wise Men" to report "on the quantities of atomic energy that can be produced in the six countries in the near future and on the means whereby this can be achieved."[8] On November 16, in what amounted to a resounding testimonial to Monnet's influence, the Community's member Governments in fact appointed Louis Armand, Franz Etzel, and the late Francesco Giordani to present "A Target for Euratom". Giordani, a thick-spectacled, bearded figure who looked like the nineteenth-century layman's idea of a scientist, was a distinguished Italian nuclear expert. Etzel, the cool lawyer and economist, was then Vice-President of the High Authority. Armand, volatile, energetic, and very French, was the brilliant scientist-engineer who had modernized the State railways, reported on atomic energy prospects to the O.E.E.C.,[9] and incidentally invented the name "Euratom". After a lightning tour of Western Europe, the United Kingdom, the United States, and Canada, they presented their report on May 4, 1957, six weeks after the signature of the Euratom Treaty.[10]

The main conclusion of the "Wise Men's" Report was that the Community face a long-term shortage of energy and that her nuclear development lagged very much behind that of the United Kingdom, the United States, and the Soviet Union. Without nuclear power, it declared, the Community's imports of energy supplies, which cost $2,000 million in 1956, would rise to $4,000 million in 1967, and might reach $6,000 million by 1975. The United States was planning to achieve a total installed nuclear capacity of 600,000 kilowatts by 1960; the Soviet Union, 2 to 2.5 million; the United Kingdom, 1.5 million by 1962. The "Wise Men" proposed that Euratom should aim at reaching 15 million kilowatts by 1967, in order to stabilize its energy imports around their expected 1963 level, at the equivalent of 165 million metric tons of hard coal.

The broad long-term picture painted by the "Wise Men" was to remain valid : but the chief significance today of its actual figures is that their impact spurred the ratification of the Euratom Treaty. When in January 1958 the Euratom Commission was installed in rue Belliard, Brussels, one of its first tasks was to refine upon much of the "Wise Men's" work. The President of the Commission was Armand himself; its Vice-President was the mercurial Enrico Medi, an Italian physicist; and its other members were Paul Hubert De Groote, a Belgian former Minister and Rector of Brussels Free University, Heinz Krekeler, a scientist who had previously been German Ambassador in Washington, and Emanuel Sassen, a Dutch former Minister and one of the most active members of the E.C.S.C.'s Common Assembly. In June, Armand already had to admit that the "Wise Men's" target was likely to be deferred, partly because of financial difficulties, new sources of oil, and the upward revision of nuclear cost estimates.[11] Despite an ambitious $350 million joint power programme with the United States, only about 1.5 million kilowatts of capacity had been authorized or was under construction by June 1961; and although this was expected to rise to 2 million kilowatts by 1965, and 40 million by 1980, Euratom's more immediate task was to prepare the way for the Community's nuclear future.

Although less spectacular than a large-scale reactor programme, this in practice meant action on several fronts at once. One of the first necessities was to stimulate and co-ordinate nuclear research. For this purpose, Euratom enjoys the advice of a highly qualified Scientific and Technical Committee, whose first President was the distinguished Italian physicist Edoardo Amaldi, and a budget of $215 million for the first five years. Its head of research is the French scientist Jules Guéron, well known to his British confrères for his atomic work in England during World War II. The current programme includes the establishment of four joint research centres—in Belgium, Germany, Italy, and the Netherlands, specific research contracts with existing private and public institutions, and collaboration with the United States, the United Kingdom, and Canada, as well as with several international organizations. To help make known the results of world research, Euratom is setting up a documentation pool which will comprise an extensive library and a special service for information on, and translations from, work published in Slavonic and Oriental languages. In the industrial field, it guides and stimulates investment by the publication of production targets and the provision of aid to reactor projects; it facilitates supplies by means of a joint Agency for raw and fissile materials, and a nuclear common market, opened on January 1, 1959; and it has prepared a nuclear insurance convention to supplement that drawn up by the members of the O.E.E.C. It has a particular responsibility, moreover, for health and safety. Here, it has drawn up a comprehensive set of basic health standards, which are binding upon the Community's member states; and it keeps a check both on the levels of radioactivity and on the safety precautions of individual projects. Finally, although it cannot, as was orginally suggested, act as a "non-nuclear club" by forbidding the member states to use nuclear energy for military purposes, it is itself exclusively concerned with the peaceful uses of the atom; and its team of inspectors maintains a regular watch on the movements of all Euratom nuclear materials to prevent their being diverted to other ends. This control system, unlike that of any existing international organization, is legally and automatically binding in the territories of the member states, and enables Euratom to obtain fissile material from the United States, for example, without having to submit to periodical visits from American Government inspectors.

These comparatively modest beginnings, of course, are no necessary foretaste of Euratom's future. Much will depend on the general energy situation and the comparative cost of nuclear power; much also on the Euratom Commission itself. During its first year, Louis Armand was a sick and over-tired man. On February 2, 1959, he was replaced by Etienne Hirsch, Monnet's former assistant and later successor on the French *Plan*, and one of those involved in the original Schuman Declaration. Hirsch, friendly, pipe-smoking, and deceptively placid and leisurely in appearance, is by temperament an active and energetic "planner" and intensely "European". His persuasive optimism did much to help the morale of Euratom over a difficult period of its existence : but his more political activities and speeches were said to have put him in bad odour with President de Gaulle's Government, led by Michel Debré; and when his term of office came up for renewal at the end of 1961 he was replaced by Monsieur Pierre Chatenet, former French Minister of the Interior.

The removal of Etienne Hirsch, who had indicated that he would be willing to remain in office, caused considerable outcry; since although France was perfectly within her rights in proposing to the other governments whatever candidate she wished, some thought that this looked suspiciously close to bringing pressure to bear upon one whose very mandate obliged him to remain free of national interests. As Hirsch put it in a typically intransigent declaration when his replacement was announced, "the French President of Euratom is not in the service of France."[12] But other member governments, whose consent was required for the change, were unwilling to bring the matter to a crisis, since to do so might have put in jeopardy the mandate of the other Brussels Executive, the Common Market Commission, also due for renewal at the end of 1961. This consideration was perhaps an index of how greatly the relative importance attached to Euratom and the Common Market had changed since 1956, when in the words of an American observer, "most 'European' strategists gave priority to the Euratom plan".[13]

Even in 1956, however, there had been criticism of extending European integration sector by sector—partly for fear that each new sector to be integrated would in turn encounter on its periphery the same kind of difficulties as those already noted in the case of coal and steel. The failure of E.D.C. had already marked a pause in the direct and explicitly political approach towards European unity : but it more especially foreshadowed the end of partial approaches by means of sector integration, except in the rather special field of nuclear energy. Looking back, I think that one may also regard this period as marking the end of a kind of "constructive opportunism"—very necessary at the time—which specialized in seizing the chance to make a breakthrough in such successively promising but limited fields as, first, the problems of German heavy industry, secondly those of German re-armament, and thirdly the European energy shortage and the comparative *tabula rasa* offered by nuclear power. From now on, profiting from a successful breakthrough, the integration movement was able to consolidate and extend itself in a much more comprehensive way. After the armoured thrust, so to speak, there followed the gradual invasion; and its instrument was what in those early days was still called the "general" Common Market.

The idea of global economic integration was not, of course, new. The Marshall Plan, as has been seen, might have led to a European customs union; and in addition to the Benelux economic union, at least two similar projects were suggested in the O.E.E.C. as early as June 1950. Giuseppe Pella, then Italian Minister of the Treasury, had proposed with the backing of his

Government a European preference zone in which tariffs between
O.E.E.C. members would be reduced as much as possible; and
although the project was essentially "co-operative" and "international", it nevertheless recognized that it might involve partial
abandonment of economic sovereignty. A second, in some ways
more thoroughgoing proposal, was that of the then Dutch
Foreign Minister Dirk Stikker, which he entitled "A plan of
action for European economic integration" : this would have
extended the O.E.E.C.'s product-by-product method, already
used in liberalizing quotas, to the elimination of tariffs between
its members. In addition to these proposals, moreover, there had
been several plans for regional economic integration. Of these,
the most elaborate was "Francita"—an Italian proposal of July
12, 1947, for a customs union with France : this assumed treaty
form on March 26, 1949, but got little further. A similar but
quicker fate befell a plan to merge "Francita" with Benelux,
under the joint name of "Fritalux" or "Finebel" : this remained
at the level of discussion among experts. No more successful were
the plans for a United Kingdom–Scandinavian and a Greco–
Turkish customs union; and the same, for obvious reasons, was
true of the proposals for a general common market prepared by
the Ad hoc Assembly as a feature of the abortive European Political Community.[14] In these ways, and in several years' experience
of the common market for coal and steel, some of the Community's future problems were already familiar when the Common Market Treaty was signed in Rome.

The Rome Treaty, obviously enough, is a negotiated document, containing concessions and counter-concessions, careful
wording, ingenious compromises, and special protocols which
settle residual details. But it would be a mistake to see it simply
as a complex of bargains. In fact, it embodies some consistent
but not doctrinaire thinking about both economics and
politics; and in many respects it closely follows Part I of the
Spaak Report of April 1956. Much of this was the work of Pierre

Uri, who already in the previous year had produced for the High
Authority a "Memorandum on General Economic Integration in
Europe" reaffirming that "full integration is the real point of the
venture in which the Schuman Plan is the first stage" and setting
forth the basic principles of such further progress.[15] Earlier still,
moreover, the beginnings of many later ideas had been outlined
during the economic discussions relating to the E.P.C. Here, the
experts of the Ad hoc Assembly had proposed a common market
for goods, capital, and persons; the co-ordination of monetary,
financial, and credit policies; and a resettlement fund similar to
that of the E.C.S.C. They had pointed out, however, that in
global integration it would be impossible to lay down all the rules
in advance, and that a large measure of discretion would have
to be left to the Community's institutions. The Ministers, in their
turn, had not discussed these recommendations in detail : but at
the senior-official level, although the French delegation was unable to commit itself, the others produced a draft which is still
interesting today. They defined a common market as being based
on the free movement of goods, capital, persons, and services. To
achieve this, they recognized that measures distorting competition
would have to be eliminated; that economic, financial, and social
policies would have to be co-ordinated; that the establishment of
the common market would have to be gradual, comprehensive,
subject to safeguards, and assisted by a resettlement and modernization fund; and finally, that a common customs and trade
policy would have to be adopted *vis-à-vis* non-member states.

In different words, all these ideas reappear in the Rome Treaty,
which is thus in part a logical development from previous efforts.
From this point of view, the Common Market might be seen as
an attempt to recover as much as possible of what was lost when
the plan for a European Political Community was abandoned,
by extending to the whole territory of its member states as many
as possible of the economic conditions that normally apply to any
single country. It is equally possible, however, to approach the

Common Market from another starting-point—that is, from the classical economic arguments for freer trade and larger markets. While the former viewpoint is useful in interpreting the Treaty, the latter approach was frequently used by its supporters during the debates on its ratification, and is therefore worth exploring in more detail.

The Common Market is based on a customs union, within which tariff barriers are to be eliminated, and around which the separate external tariffs of the member states are to be averaged out into a common tariff *vis-à-vis* the rest of the world. A free trade area, by contrast, is one in which internal tariffs are eliminated, but member countries each retain their own external tariffs. While such an arrangement imposes fewer obligations on them, it also means that there will be a tendency for imports from the outside world to be routed through the lower-tariff countries even when they are destined for those maintaining higher external tariffs. Besides depriving the latter's ports of some of their accustomed traffic, such diversion of trade is clearly uneconomic, since it means that the goods in question will be making an unnecessary journey: moreover, by side-stepping the external frontier of the country they are intended for, they make nonsense of the higher tariff that they thus evade. If tariff differences are sufficient to make such diversion of trade profitable to traders, the only remedy may be to establish special certificates showing the origin of goods that circulate within the free trade area, and to impose compensatory levies on those imported into a higher-tariff country via one of its lower-tariff neighbours. It was partly to avoid such complications that the Community countries rejected the formula of a free trade area when framing the Rome Treaty, and adopted that of a customs union instead.

To be effective, however, a customs union cannot confine its scope to tariffs. It must also tackle quantitative restrictions, the second traditional barrier to trade; and just as its members apply a common tariff in their trade with non-member countries, so they must apply a common trade policy. Tariffs and quantitative restrictions, moreover, are only the most obvious means whereby twentieth-century Governments may protect home markets and industries and thereby restrict trade. Another is the granting of subsidies which artificially lower the costs of home industry and act as a barrier to imports by making them less competitive. Taxation systems, legislative requirements, and even professional qualifications may similarly be manipulated to give undue favour to the home producer; and for certain products, especially heavy goods, transport rates may be used for the same purpose, either by discriminating against foreign freight or foreign users, or by imposing so-called "terminal charges" for the crossing of frontiers, out of proportion to whatever real costs the operation may involve. When itself tackling the problem, the E.C.S.C. High Authority had discovered that certain state railways imposed charges for loading and unloading at frontiers, even when the train did not stop.

Nor is it only publicly imposed barriers that have to be removed. Firms, too, may distort or hamper competition. They may artificially improve their competitive position in a neighbouring country by "dumping" their goods on its market at sales prices lower than those charged at home. They may come together with their competitors in market-sharing agreements that restrict trade and divide the common market, or in cartels and price rings that artificially protect less efficient producers by keeping everyone's prices unduly high. Monopolies, likewise, may act in the same way as cartels. In all these fields, therefore, the Common Market must keep the frontiers open and preserve competitive freedom.

But this freedom, in its turn, cannot be limited to the movement of goods alone. To enjoy all the advantages of the larger market, it is equally necessary to liberalize the other factors of production—capital and persons—and the services which they supply. Current payments must obviously be freed to enable freely moving commodities to be paid for; and investments must be freed to enable capital to migrate to wherever it will be most productive. The same applies to the movement of people—not only to allow labour, business, and the professions to be most economically located, but also to give human beings the fundamental right to choose where they wish to work.

In all these ways, one aspect of the Common Market is therefore a thorough dismantling of national economic barriers. Here, in the eyes of the Treaty-makers, there were two particular lessons to be drawn from the experience of the E.C.S.C. The first was that time would be needed to adjust to the new situation. The Rome Treaty therefore provides for a transition period, during which the barriers are gradually to come down and national policies *vis-à-vis* the rest of the world are to be aligned. Secondly, if adjustments are to be made purposefully, the time for doing so cannot be unlimited : the barriers must come down according to a timetable, so that people know where they stand; and they must come down permanently. Few industrialists are likely to adapt their production plant to the needs and opportunities of the larger area if there remains a danger that one day the barriers may go up again and their market once more shrink to merely national proportions. For this reason, the Common Market's transition period was set at twelve years, with regular reductions of tariffs and regular measures to relax quantitative restrictions : it may not be prolonged for more than fifteen years, and thereafter there is no going back. Whereas the E.C.S.C. Treaty was signed for fifty years, both the Rome Treaties are of indefinite duration.

The experience of the E.C.S.C., moreover, suggested a third conclusion. Pierre Uri expressed it thus : "Provided that a sufficiently rapid rate of expansion be maintained, there is no real difficulty in a process of integration : there is no unemployment, there are no—or there are few—shutdowns of firms."[16] He was speaking in 1957; and if the example of the steel boom proved his point, the coal crisis of the following year was to stress the importance of his proviso. In pure free trading theory, expansion would no doubt have been presumed to follow automatically upon the removal of national trade barriers : but despite the aspects of the Common Market Treaty so far described, it is not by any means a modern reincarnation of Adam Smith. It is more, in fact, than just an advanced form of customs union, for it calls in addition for positive policies to replace the famous "hidden hand". The first Article of the Treaty includes among its aims "a continuous and balanced expansion" and "an increased stability", and, as one of the means to this, "progressively approximating the economic policies of member states". The word "balanced" here is particularly important. A common market may well require some degree of imbalance between its members in various sectors in order to give it the necessary dynamism; but the cases of imbalance must not be so distributed as to put one or more of the member countries at a permanent disadvantage, and they must not be so great as to get out of hand. Finally, this is bound to involve a much closer co-ordination of economic, financial, and monetary policies than is expressly provided for in the Treaty.

Even as it is, the Treaty calls for a number of special measures which substantially depart from the pure philosophy of free competition. One such instance is that of agriculture, where merely dismantling trade barriers would simply lead to chaos and hardship : here, a managed market is gradually to be introduced, and a programme of structural reform is planned. Another example is transport, which in the Messina Resolution was treated separately from general economic integration, and which fills a special "Title" or chapter in the Rome Treaty. Here again, a mere reliance on free competition, without a clear-cut policy, would never solve all the difficulties.

In three other instances, moreover, the Treaty provides for special aid to facilitate adjustment to the Common Market, and specifies that this shall be financed on a Community basis. The first, partly modelled on the E.C.S.C. resettlement fund, is the

European Social Fund for the retraining and resettlement of workpeople : it reimburses half of the expenses incurred in this field by member states on projects approved by the Common Market Commission. The second is the $1,000-million European Investment Bank, which may help to finance modernization or new activities of general Community interest: one of its main rôles is to aid regional development, by helping to provide the necessary economic infrastructure in the Community's backward areas.

The third form of special aid is that offered to the Community countries' former colonies, of which the greater part are now independent African states. This was not mentioned in the Messina Resolution, although a hint of it had appeared in the Schuman Declaration and it had been debated by the Ad hoc Assembly; and in fact it was only late in the preparations for the Common Market—first at Venice in May 1956, and subsequently at a special meeting in Paris in the following February—that the question was raised by France. Nevertheless, the Rome Treaty provides for the gradual establishment of what is virtually a free trade area between the Community as a whole and the colonies and ex-colonies of its member states; and because this by itself could not provide the necessary stimulus to economic growth, it is supplemented by a Development Fund with $581.25 million at its disposal for the first five years. These arrangements, whereby Germany, with no ex-colonies, makes as big a contribution as France, whose former colonies are the chief beneficiaries, gave rise to some criticism during parliamentary debates on the Treaty. Not unnaturally, however, the scheme is popular with the recipients of the Community's aid; and it also has some logic to recommend it. If the ex-colonies had not been thus "associated" with the Common Market, it would still have been necessary to decide whether or not their produce should continue to enjoy preferential entry into France. Had it done so, this might well have led to a diversion of trade which is now forestalled by the gradual establishment of direct free entry into the whole of the Community.

Since the volume of trade in question is fairly limited, it seems unlikely to have serious ill-effects on the other member countries, who in any case are not themselves producers of most of the commodities concerned. Similarly, since the Community involves a pooling of problems as well as of resources, it was logical, if shrewd, of France to request help from her partners in her already extensive programme of economic aid for Africa.

Such, very briefly, were the general economic ideas underlying the Common Market Treaty. There remained the question of its institutions. In a heated debate in May 1956 before the E.C.S.C.'s Common Assembly, Michel Debré, at that time an extremely articulate and critical delegate from the French Senate, accused the Spaak Committee of having among other things forced the Common Market and Euratom into "the Procrustean bed of the E.C.S.C. institutions."[17] In a pulverizing speech, Spaak denied the charges, and claimed that the Committee had reached its conclusions without preconceived ideas. It is difficult, perhaps, not to feel some sympathy with Monsieur Debré's criticism : but the institutional structure provided for the Common Market could certainly be justified, if only by the successful experience of the Coal and Steel Community.

It was necessary, first of all, to establish an independent Community Executive, not only to safeguard the interests of the Community as such and to take a certain number of decisions, but also to act as initiator and advocate of the detailed Community legislation that would be necessary to put the Treaty's principles into practice. In the Common Market, this rôle was assigned to the nine-man Commission, whose members were appointed in January 1958. Like the nine members of the High Authority and the five of the Euratom Commission, the Common Market Commissioners are not national representatives : they are forbidden, once appointed, to accept or solicit instructions. Appointed to the Presidency was Walter Hallstein, the law Professor and former German Secretary of State for Foreign Affairs

who had headed the German delegation in the E.C.S.C. negotiations and represented his country at Messina. The Vice-Presidents
were Sicco L. Mansholt, the tall, bronzed former Dutch Minister
of Agriculture who in 1950 had proposed an agricultural common market in the O.E.E.C.; the burly Piero Malvestiti, later to
become President of the High Authority; and Robert Marjolin,
the incisive French economist who had been Monnet's colleague
on the *Plan* before becoming the O.E.E.C.'s first Secretary-
General. The other members of the Commission were Hans von
der Groeben, who had headed the German delegation negotiating
the Rome Treaties and had been co-author of the Spaak Report;
Robert Lemaignen, a senior French industrialist with long experience of public affairs; Giuseppe Petrilli, a distinguished Italian
university expert on economic and social matters; Michel Rasquin, the veteran federalist and Socialist leader from Luxembourg; and Jean Rey, the energetic and affable Belgian who as
Minister for Economic Affairs had frequently been President of
the E.C.S.C.'s Council of Ministers.[18]

Independent of the member states and therefore of the national
parliaments, the Commission, like the High Authority before it,
had clearly to be subject to democratic control. For this purpose,
the 78-member Common Assembly was replaced by a 142-man
Assembly common to all three Community organizations. Its
power to dismiss the High Authority was extended to cover the
Euratom and Common Market Commissions; and it was further
given the right to scrutinize the budgets of the new institutions,
which for the time being were not to be independently financed,
like the High Authority, but covered by joint payments from the
member states. For the time being, too, the new Assembly was
still to be appointed by and from the national parliaments; but it
was asked to propose a system of direct elections. In practice, it
looked very much like a larger version of the old Common
Assembly : it had the same Secretariat, and many of the same
members. At its inaugural meeting in Strasbourg in March 1958

it showed its mettle by refusing to elect an Italian to its Presidency, as the Ministers, anxious to preserve the balance of nationalities, had suggested. Instead, it chose Robert Schuman, and re-baptized itself "the European Parliament". Its ambitions match its name.[19]

Subject to democratic control, the Community Executives had also to be subject to the rule of law. Law, in this instance, meant chiefly the quasi-constitutional law enshrined in the Treaties; and this in turn prompted the establishment of a quasi-constitutional court. The Court of Justice of the E.C.S.C. was therefore transformed into a supreme Court to serve all three Community organizations; but although it now had a new President, the youthful Dutch jurist Andreas Donner, it maintained continuity with its predecessor not only by inheriting forty-five of its predecessor's cases, but also by retaining all but two of its other Judges, as well as its Clerk and its two Advocates-General. It held its inaugural ceremony in Luxembourg in October 1958.

The overall structure of the Community's institutions had finally, of course, to be completed by linking it more closely with the economies and the governments of the member states. In the field of labour, industry, business, and the professions, this was achieved by the inclusion of representatives of these interests on a 101-member Economic and Social Committee—a kind of legitimized pressure group which has to be consulted on a large number of major issues : for coal and steel the Consultative Committee, with fifty-one members, plays a similar rôle. At governmental level, the link is formed by the Council of Ministers, which under the Rome Treaties has a much more prominent position than in the E.C.S.C., since its vote is required for important decisions, if only because the Common Market Treaty—and in some degree the Euratom Treaty too—are "framework laws" whose details have to be filled in by just such decisions as time goes on. In the E.C.S.C. meetings of the Council were prepared, as they still are, by a Co-ordinating Committee of national senior officials, meeting shortly before the Ministers : under the Rome Treaties, a standing Committee of Permanent Representatives, accredited to the Community by its member states, with Ambassadorial rank, has the far more formidable task of processing the mass of detailed documents, sounding out national positions and possibilities of agreement, and maintaining close liaison with the Community Executives. Initially, there was some apprehension lest the Permanent Representatives, whose Committee is of course purely "inter-governmental", should come to assume a preponderant rôle in the new Community organizations, thereby sapping their "European" structure : but in fact relations with the Common Market and Euratom Executives are more cordial than was originally feared, and although the Permanent Representatives remain national spokesmen, bound by their governments' instructions, they cannot help but be infected by a sense of common purpose. The Council, moreover, remains the forum for decisions, and these may in many cases—and increasingly as the transition period progresses—be taken by majority vote. What is more, the Council can normally decide only upon proposals from the Commission, and can only amend such proposals if all its members unanimously agree on the amendment. In this way, although the Commission's "powers" are less than those of the High Authority, its actual influence is very much greater—in particular because the field covered by the Common Market is so vast, and because the task of its institutions, in part at least, is to produce within the Rome Treaty's framework new and detailed agreements between the member states, not unlike a series of sequels to the original Schuman Plan.

In the early days of the Community, when the E.C.S.C. stood alone, it was the novel institutional aspect of European integration that attracted most attention as a factor for "political" unity. Personally, I believe that the "supranationalism" of the E.C.S.C. can easily be overstressed : but it would be equally mistaken to underestimate that of the Common Market. In all three

Community organizations, indeed, the institutional framework is still vital to success; what makes it seem less striking now is the fact that it has become familiar. Once the Community's novel institutions are accepted, in fact, it becomes very clear that they are by no means its only "political" feature. In the words of the Schuman Declaration, already quoted, an economic community introduces "the germ of a broader and deeper community" by creating "*de facto* solidatity". Nor is it merely a preparation for political unity, for in many respects it is already "political" itself. Although its subject-matter is primarily economic, its work chiefly concerns economic policy; and although the semantic connexion between "policy" and "politics" is more evident in French, German, Italian, and Dutch, where the words "*politique*", "*Politik*", "*politica*", and "*politiek*" are all used for both, the two notions are not entirely separate even in English. As Professor Hallstein has put it, "What is being integrated is the part played by the national states in creating the conditions within which economic activity takes place.... It is not just a movement for free trade between separate economies. It is a movement to fuse markets— and economies—into one. . . . Is this not a far-reaching political commitment?" It was this line of reasoning that led to the often-quoted conclusion, "We are not in business—we are in politics."[20]

Superficially, it is tempting to regard the shift from the "break-through" technique of the Schuman Declaration to the global approach of the Common Market as the expression of a difference in temperament between Jean Monnet and Walter Hallstein —between the French "live-wire" and the German law Professor; between the hero of a runaway marriage and the lifelong bachelor; between the daring, sometimes incautious political activist, and the patient multilingual intellectual giant whose present task is economic integration; between the small hand-picked team of the Avenue Foch and the 1,900-strong Common Market Commission staff of the Avenue de la Joyeuse Entrée, Brussels. But the contrast is largely artificial; and especially as regards staffing it is much more a matter of functions than of personalities. In fact, Professor Hallstein is far from the stereotype of the academic jurist : he has a very wide range of general interests, including music, the theatre, and sculpture (of which he has some interesting modern specimens in his office); and despite his studious appearance he possesses a warm and idiosyncratic sense of humour, which off duty is capable of quite extraordinary saturnalian high spirits. Characteristically, his car is a grey convertible, and he has several times caught colds through driving with the hood down in unsuitable weather. In policy matters he is usually cautious, and, a shy man, will never play to the gallery; but he sometimes takes calculated risks. Like Monnet, he is a convinced and dedicated European, whose whole post-war career has been bound up with the integration movement. Like Monnet, he has an inspiring vision of what European unity could achieve, but he keeps both feet firmly on the ground. It is no coincidence that the two men still keep closely in touch.

Monnet may have been instrumental in securing the ratification of the Rome Treaties; but Hallstein certainly deserves much of the credit for the prestige and success of the Common Market so far. Obviously, it is still too early to draw up a balance-sheet. In its first four years of activity, the Community has only just begun to reach the points where integration hurts; and there may be many headaches to come. The difficulty with which agreement was reached on agricultural policy at the end of 1961 and the beginning of 1962 made it clear that continued, detailed efforts, and a continuing political will to find solutions, will be necessary in this field for several years ahead. The same will be true of general, economic, financial, and monetary policy, where the Treaty's provisions are extremely flexible; and similar determination will no doubt be needed to solve the problems of a common energy policy and of harmonizing national legislation in the competition field.

Nevertheless, in its first four years the Common Market has

scored some successes, not the least of them being its triumphant passage into stage two of the transition period, agreed at 5.29 a.m. on January 14, 1962, after an all-night session of the Council of Ministers devoted to hammering out agreement on agriculture, the fruit of weeks of work. Its first series of internal tariff cuts, and the first levelling-out of national external tariffs, have been achieved ahead of schedule, while quantitative restrictions on industrial products have almost disappeared. At the same time, the first steps have been taken to free the other factors of production. May 1960 saw the removal of a first series of restrictions on the free movement of capital. In June 1961 the Community set its first timetable for removing restrictions on the movement of labour; and in October 1961 it approved an elaborate double programme which will ultimately enable any citizen of the Community, and any firm established within it, to do business, exercise a profession, or supply services, anywhere thoughout the area. In June 1960 the first rules against transport discrimination were published : in December 1961, the first regulations on cartels.

Looking to future economic development, the Common Market Commission has envisaged a 4 to 5 per cent annual increase in the gross national product. To aid steady and balanced growth, the Community has established a trade-cycle policy committee alongside the Monetary Committee set up by the Treaty, and has made a start on its regional policy by convening an expert conference on the subject in December 1961. By that date, the European Investment Bank had made loans totalling $120.5 million, nearly 70 per cent of them in Italy. On energy policy, a joint group representing the three Community Executives proposed a programme of immediate action early in 1961, and is working on longer-term proposals. Later in the year, the Common Market Commission put forward its first suggestions for a common transport policy. The European Social Fund was brought into effect in 1960, with a budget of $30 million for that year and 1961. Already in 1958, working on the E.C.S.C.'s experience, the Community had adopted a joint system of social security for migrant workers; in December 1961 it agreed that equal pay for men and women would become law in all Community countries by the end of 1964. The Commission's first proposals for agricultural policy were submitted in the summer of 1960, and were approved early in 1962. Finally, the Development Fund for the associated overseas countries and territories had allocated a good half of its total resources by the end of 1961, and the Community had held a first meeting with the now independent African states with a view to remodelling the form of their Association with the Common Market. Clearly, the 1,900 members of the staff had not been exactly idle.

The one subject of their activities, however, which had attracted the most outside attention was something that strangely enough did not enjoy a chapter to itself in the Rome Treaty. This was the subject of the Community's relations with the rest of the world. As one of the negotiators of the Treaty put it, "We were very naïve at Val Duchesse : we thought that all our difficulties would come from pressure groups within the Common Market. We had no idea that the very size of the undertaking would create difficulties outside as well". If this was true, it was naïve indeed. Eight months after the Rome Treaty was signed, its protagonists found themselves arguing in the G.A.T.T. with several non-European countries who feared that it might damage their exports; and eight months before the Treaty's signature, the O.E.E.C. had echoed to the first rumblings of similar disquiet in Europe. One key to this problem was the future relationship between the nascent Community and Great Britain.

CHAPTER VII

PERPLEXED ALBION: THE BRITISH DILEMMA

Is Great Britain part of Europe? To an American visitor, the answer is usually obvious: but an Englishman would certainly hesitate before replying. The roots of his uncertainty go deep; and in order to understand British policy *vis-à-vis* the European Community, it is necessary to see how Britain was affected by the pre-history of European integration.

Of the many political influences that coloured continental Europe, not all left so deep a mark upon the British Isles. Despite the Roman occupation, Roman Law was never fully accepted. Despite the fact that William the Conqueror called himself *"rex Norm-Anglorum"* ("King of the Anglo-Normans"), his successors became *"rex Anglorum"* ("King of the English") or *"rex Anglie"* ("King of England"): by 1394, Norman French in England was so remote from its continental counterpart that negotiators could only understand each other by writing down what they had to say.[1] Despite King Richard I's example—or perhaps because of it—Crusading was never widely popular in England; and Clause 7 of the "Unknown Charter" which preceded Magna Carta sought to restrict knight-service abroad.[2] Despite the influence of the medieval Empire, it never subdued the English kingdom; and despite England's rôle in Christianizing part of continental Europe during the Dark Ages, the medieval Papacy even in its heyday never fully curbed the sense of independence in the English Church. The Reformation made the split deeper, and partly for this reason there was perhaps less widespread nostalgia in England for a medieval unity in which the country had not fully shared. For England, indeed, Tudor prosperity made a happy contrast with the Wars of the Roses. In the following century, while Germany was still plunged in the Thirty Years' War, England was engaged in her own Civil War —the last, *Deo volente*, to be fought on her soil. In the eighteenth century, European cosmopolitanism certainly extended to the British Isles : but ever since the revocation of the Edict of Nantes in 1685 they had played a rather special rôle as a haven for refugees. Voltaire, himself one such exile, declared that "the English nation is the only one on earth that has managed to regulate the power of kings by resisting them, and which by successive efforts has finally established this wise government where the sovereign, all-powerful to do good, has his hands tied if he wishes to do evil, where the nobility is great without insolence and without vassals, and where the people partake in government without confusion".[3]

From the vantage-point of so happy a situation, some Englishmen were bound to view the American Revolution rather differently from their neighbours on the continent. The establishment of the United States in the new world, far from seeming a precedent for some United States of Europe, appeared rather in the nature of a colonial revolt; and some held a similarly unfavourable view of the Revolution in France. Napoleon, in his turn, if he helped to unite the continent, merely united Englishmen against him; and it was well said that the gospel of Rousseau which in France produced the Terror, in England produced *Sandford and Merton*. English Romanticism, in fact, was predominantly literary, not political. Finally, while continental socialism undoubtedly spread its influence in Great Britain, its federalist aspects never had widespread appeal. "Federalism," said Dicey with chilling authority, "substitutes litigation for legislation."[4]

All this meant that early plans for European unity evoked

comparatively little sympathy on the far side of the Channel. This may have been partly due to lack of knowledge; for foreign visitors, although often impressed, like Voltaire, by English manners and institutions, were also frequently astonished both by what one of them termed the "British is Best" aspect of Englishmen's unspoken assumptions, and by their comparative ignorance of continental Europe. "The English politicians," wrote one such observer, ". . . do not know much more about conditions on the Continent than we know about conditions in Peru or Siam."[5] An Englishman might have returned the compliment: but one clear reason for Great Britain's aloofness was that the balance of power remained a cornerstone of her European policy, perhaps partly because it gave her the opportunity to act as a third force. Her traditional reaction to the formation of any powerful bloc in Europe was to throw her own weight into the balance against it; and when Napoleon was followed by Kaiser Wilhelm II and Adolf Hitler, habit was confirmed in the one case by reason and in the other by common humanity.

Political considerations of this sort were partly influenced and partly reinforced by geographical and economic facts. The importance of Great Britain's being an island is so obvious that it is not always stated. Psychologically, a land frontier is much less imposing than even a narrow strip of water: before the days of aircraft, indeed, it was practically impossible for English travellers —unless they took a train ferry—to climb into the same vehicle in their own country as they would later alight from in another. As an island, moreover, Great Britain had early developed her navy; and her maritime successes helped her to enjoy the pick of the temperate areas outside Europe, in which her own emigrants founded "white" colonies which kept strong links with home, whereas after the Seven Years' War the French colonies, for example, were much more confined to tropical zones. Britain's mercantile prosperity later helped her to win the lead in the Industrial Revolution, and hence to be an early protagonist of free trade. Even when the "colonial frontier" had come to an end, and Europe's relative place in the world was fast declining, Britain was still in a favourable enough position to need to make no immediate psychological or material adjustment. Her chief response to the 1929 crash was to systematize and extend the beginnings of Imperial Preference, whereby she and her overseas possessions and partners accorded each other more favourable tariff treatment than they granted the rest of the world. Linking scattered and in some ways complementary economies, the Imperial Preference system principally resembled an exercise in regional free trade rather than a case of economic integration, despite the fact that it almost coincided with the Sterling Area, whose members made use of the London banking system to discharge their international balance of payments. With the British Isles as the Empire's industrial workshop and banker, and the overseas areas as its home farm, this worked extremely well—at least until the home farm began to seek extra markets and to wish to develop its own industries, and the banker found that his own stability began to be jeopardized by his partner's fluctuating fortunes.

As the world's greatest trading nation, incapable of self-sufficiency in food production, it was for a long time Britain's interest, therefore, as well as her instinct, to look outwards over the ocean rather than across the Channel to the continent. Two world wars only served to confirm this tendency. Twice in a lifetime, Englishmen saw the continent of Europe overrun and its countries brought to the verge of destruction; and although they fought and died on the continent, their families remained at home. Sheltered by the Channel, they might be bombed, but at least they were not invaded: despite the horrors of the Blitz, English children in 1945 did not retort, like the little girl at the Pestalozzi Children's Village in Switzerland, "You tell us there are fairies in the woods—but that's not true: there are soldiers with guns".[6]

For many continental Europeans, then, World War II had discredited ideas of national sovereignty: for Englishmen with memories of 1940, it had been their triumphant vindication. The feeling of distinctness from Europe was emphasized, moreover, by the experience of the American alliance. Readers of General de Gaulle's war memoirs will recall his irritation with an Anglo-American intimacy from which he felt himself excluded; and this relationship, aided as it was by the fact of a common language, was one of the pillars on which postwar British governments sought to build a stable peace. Only when the United States began to show signs of wishing to treat Great Britain as a senior but not unique member of the European family did this factor begin to lose weight.

One further element in the postwar situation remains to be mentioned. The Labour Party's landslide electoral victory in 1945 seemed to its sympathizers to promise fulfilment of all the hopes that they had nursed during the war—for social justice and welfare at home, and for worldwide peace abroad. The task of rebuilding Britain on a new model and of fashioning a new international society in the United Nations seemed far more urgent than the creation of some regional organization in Western Europe. Two years later, when the beginnings of the "cold war" were beginning to chill the prospect of an effectively united world, Europe desperately needed all the help that Britain could give her : but Britain herself was in the same case. Addressing the Trades Union Congress at Southport in September 1947, Ernest Bevin sounded almost in despair : "Even since I have been in office," he said, "I have been wondering and wondering what I could do or put to my colleagues in the Cabinet by which we could assist in the rehabilitation of Europe first. . . . There was not a Minister could give me anything. . . . For two years I have not had one single vote of credit in the House of Commons to assist in the rehabilitation work overseas. . . . I cannot do it alone."[7]

It was not out of ill-will, therefore, or short-sighted "insularity" that Great Britain failed, as she is often criticized for failing, to take the lead in the movement for uniting Europe after World War II. History, geography, tradition, the fortunes of war, the facts of the wartime alliance, and the hopes of a new and peaceful world—all played their part in determining her policy; and if that policy was mistaken, the mistake was natural and even in some ways noble. It led, however, to a series of suspicions on both sides of the Channel—to accusations by one side that continental Europeans were trying to do Britain down, and counter-accusations by the other that "perfidious Albion" was trying to sabotage the aim of unity in Europe. My own belief, for what it is worth, is that much of what was thought to be Machiavellian tactics in each case was simple misunderstanding. "A good deal that we interpret as deceit," wrote a former Austrian Ambassador in London, "is in fact merely the result of ignorance and superficiality, and is due to carelessness and confusion." His words still have the ring of truth.[8]

The trouble began, as has been seen, with the proposal for a European customs union as the basis of the O.E.E.C. It was repeated when Bevin sought to avoid establishing an Assembly for the Council of Europe, and succeeded only in ensuring that the Assembly had no power. In both cases, continental Europeans had hoped for institutions that would be strong and more than merely "international" : in both cases, Britain had opted for something weaker and looser. This was the beginning of what looks in retrospect almost like a ritual dance : but for some time it was obscured by polite ambiguities, particularly in the early debates of the Council of Europe. Here, in August 1949, Mr. Maurice Edelman, one of the British Labour Party representatives, launched the term "functionalism", later to be linked with the slogan already quoted, "limited functions but real powers". These expressions seemed to satisfy both those who hoped for a strong organization to accomplish concrete tasks and those who wanted such tasks to be performed by purely traditional inter-governmental bodies. Not until the following year, however, was any serious analysis of these very different meanings attempted. The Schuman Plan, which its sponsors no doubt regarded as "functional" in the former sense, was the stumbling-block on which the ambiguity was to be broken.

The full story of the Labour Government's reaction to the Schuman Declaration has yet to be written; and it is still not clear whether Mr. Attlee would have accepted the French offer to begin negotiations even had Great Britain not been required to pledge herself in advance to a "supranational" High Authority. Certainly, there were voices for and against in the Party : but what is relevant here is that both the Government, in private, and Mr. Eccles and Mr. Macmillan, speaking at the Council of Europe as members of the Conservative Opposition, made counter-proposals that would have considerably watered down the original Schuman Plan, transforming it into a largely inter-governmental arrangement of more traditional design.[9] Later, likewise, when Monnet proposed a close form of association be-tween the E.C.S.C. and Great Britain, with efforts to reduce mutual trade barriers, the eventual result was a rather looser agreement providing chiefly for joint consultation.

A similar pattern emerged in the case of E.D.C. By now, a Conservative government was in office; and memories of Mr. Churchill's Zurich speech of 1946, of his "European army" speech of August 1950, and of Opposition attacks on the Labour Government's reaction to the Schuman proposal, led many con-tinental Europeans to hope that Britain would now join in serious negotiations. But on the very day that Sir David Maxwell Fyfe, the then Home Secretary, announced to the Council of Europe that Britain welcomed E.D.C. and that her "possible association" with it might—although he could not promise it—"lead to complete and unqualified partnership", Mr. Eden, speaking in Rome, stated flatly that Britain would not join.[10]

Association was as much as she could offer; but although the
latter commitment was real, it was not enough to save the
European Defence Community.

Meanwhile, the almost ritual pattern was repeated once more.
Dismayed by reactions to his Rome statement, Mr. Eden produced a further proposal, which later came to be known as "the
Eden Plan". Mr. Anthony Nutting, at that time Parliamentary
Under-Secretary of State for Foreign Affairs, has described very
vividly how at a meeting in Paris in March 1952 the Committee
of Ministers of the Council of Europe reacted—apparently very
warmly—to Eden's exposition of his plan : but Nutting's own
description of the scheme makes the sceptical reader of his
account wonder whether the smiles of the Ministers were wholly
lacking in irony. "The essence of the plan," he says, ". . . was to
make the Council of Europe the parent body. . . . The Committee
of Ministers, the Assembly and the Secretariat of the Council of
Europe would become the Committee of Ministers, the Assembly
and the Secretariat [sic] of the Coal and Steel Pool and the
E.D.C." He goes on to accuse Jean Monnet of having "sabo-
taged" this proposal—although the terms in which he himself
describes it suggest some misunderstanding of the nature of the
E.C.S.C.[11]

It would be unfair, however, to ignore the substantial contribution that both Eden and his advisers made when E.D.C.
collapsed. Western European Union, Eden's own brain-child,
undoubtedly helped to save the day when all seemed lost; and if
W.E.U., like the "Eden Plan", again seemed to follow the pattern
already described, this time the ritual had some purpose and
some content.

Unfortunately, the misunderstanding between Great Britain
and continental Europe now seemed to be becoming mutual. To
Britain herself, it no doubt seemed as if over the past years continental Europeans had forever been preparing a kind of union

so tight as to exclude anyone with wider interests and responsibilities who was not willing to accept strong common institutions and common policies. It no doubt seemed quite natural for her to seek a compromise by counter-proposing each time some looser framework in which she felt she could participate, without making the basic change of attitude and policy that the "European" activists demanded of her. But this in turn made it seem on the other side of the Channel as if Great Britain, although for understandable reasons, was treating the new forms of political and economic life that Europeans were trying to evolve to meet new situations simply as traditional bids in the game of international diplomacy, to be met each time by counter-bids leading to something much less ambitious.

The melancholy history of these proposals and counter-proposals helps to explain the basic political difficulties which arose around the Common Market and the plan for a European Free Trade Area. Here once again it looked as if Great Britain was merely repeating the same old tactics. In June 1955, she had been invited to the Messina Conference. The story of how it came about that she was not represented is another piece of history that still remains to be written; but she was nevertheless represented on the Spaak Committee, again by special invitation. During the autumn of 1955, her representative contributed a great deal to its technical discussions, and for a short time it looked as if all was well. In December, however, it appears that the question of political commitments was raised unequivocally, and British representation was withdrawn. In the following July, however, when the Spaak Report had been accepted by the Ministers of the Community countries, and negotiations had started, Britain now proposed that an O.E.E.C. working party be appointed to study the possibility of establishing a Free Trade Area embracing all the O.E.E.C. countries and including the Common Market as one of its members. In the following January, after a report from the working party, the O.E.E.C. Council agreed to begin negotiations "in order to determine ways and means on the basis of which" such a Free Trade Area "could be brought into being".[12]

The terms of this decision reveal already a degree of scepticism rather than full agreement on the aim to be achieved: but in the early days of the Free Trade Area negotiations scepticism was certainly tempered by hope. I myself was present in January 1958 when Walter Hallstein, who had then been President of the Common Market Commission for just a week, recorded a radio interview in which he declared: "I personally think that the Free Trade Area is a necessary supplement to the Common Market."[13] True, he went on to qualify this statement, laying particular emphasis on relations with Great Britain and the United States; but in the previous October the whole Council of the O.E.E.C.—although in the absence of a French Government—had recorded its members' "determination to secure the establishment of a European Free Trade Area", and it was only gradually that a more reserved attitude began to develop.[14] As the months wore on, however, it became clear that success was eluding the negotiators; and already in the summer of 1958 the Common Market Commission suggested that alternative interim arrangements might be made to cushion the effect on the Community's partners of the first steps towards the full Common Market, due on January 1, 1959. It was not until November 1958 that Jacques Soustelle, then French Minister of Information, bluntly announced what many had long been suspecting— that "it is not possible to create the Free Trade Area as wished by the British", with no common external tariff and no harmonization in the economic and social spheres.[15] Continental Press reactions were unexcited, but British newspapers next morning carried the story under massive, gloomy headlines, and two days later Mr. Reginald Maudling, British chairman of the negotiating committee, indefinitely postponed its next meeting. All was over bar the shouting, of which one of the loudest examples was a strongly worded *Times* first leader entitled "France the Wrecker".[16]

Apart from the technical difficulty of reconciling a loose Free Trade Area with a much tighter and more far-reaching Common Market, the failure of the negotiations was due both to conflicts of interest and to real difficulties of conception. In 1958, the charge of "French protectionism" still had some validity : but so had the fear that Great Britain, at the crossroads of Commonwealth Preference and a largely industrial free trade system in Europe, would enjoy advantages denied to some of her European partners. The economic philosophy underlying the Free Trade Area concept seemed to aggravate this problem by failing to take account of the other measures of economic co-operation and even integration that would be necessary even to achieve the traditional objectives of free trade; and at the same time, by seeming to offer classical free trade without strong institutions and economic discipline, the Free Trade Area threatened to tempt some Common Market members away from the stricter concept of economic integration at a time when the new Community was still very young. This danger was increased by the disruptive effect of the Community's negotiating not as one entity but as six single states, each subject to bilateral pressure through traditional diplomatic channels. Finally, and more especially as time went on and the United States began to suffer from a balance-of-payments problem, it began to seem unhelpful to establish O.E.E.C.-wide tariff discrimination against the dollar area just at the moment when Europe's own balance-of-payments situation was making possible and indeed demanding the removal of quota discrimination. Although this last argument may sometimes have been advanced for partly tactical reasons by those who disliked the Free Trade Area on other grounds as well, it nevertheless had increasing importance as European countries moved towards convertibility of their currencies at the end of 1958; and it corresponded fairly enough to official attitudes in

Washington, which although scrupulously neutral during the Free Trade negotiations, had always made it clear that the United States, while accepting a measure of trade discrimination by the Common Market, did so only in return for the political advantages of real unity in Europe.

Much time and many tempers were lost in exchanging these arguments when the Free Trade Area negotiations broke down. However, anxious to proceed unchallenged with its first internal tariff cuts and quota enlargements, the Community made conciliatory gestures by extending to its O.E.E.C. partners some—but, on principle, not all—of these first mutual concessions on the way to the full Common Market. It also proposed to follow a generally liberal policy *vis-à-vis* all G.A.T.T. members, to establish a "contact committee" to discuss specific trade difficulties with its European partners, and to consult with Great Britain, the United States, and Canada on the co-ordination of economic policies and of aid to developing countries. It added that these proposals would be furthered by greater consolidation of the Common Market itself, a suggestion echoed during the summer of 1959 by several plans—including that of Monsieur Pierre Wigny, then Belgian Foreign Minister—for an acceleration of its transition period. This proposal was finally accepted on May 12, 1960.[17] In deciding to accelerate the realization of the Common Market, and hence of its common external tariff, the Community also agreed to a partial and provisional 20 per cent cut in the tariff, to anticipate the G.A.T.T. negotiations already proposed by C. Douglas Dillon, then U.S. Under-Secretary of State for Economic Affairs, which had been accepted by the Community in May 1959. All this was a clear attempt to take the heat off the wider European debate by diminishing "discrimination" all round.

Meanwhile, however, events in the rest of Europe had been moving rapidly. In June and July 1959 respectively, Greece and Turkey had requested "association" with the Common Market

in default of the wider Free Trade Area; and at about the same
time Great Britain had been forming the European Free Trade
Association (E.F.T.A.) or "Outer Seven", comprising herself,
Austria, Denmark, Norway, Portugal, Sweden, and Switzerland.[18]
Already in December 1958 some such scheme had been mooted
at a meeting between the British and Swedish Federations of
Industry, to be taken up on the civil-service level in February
and March 1959. Accepted in draft form by Ministers in July,
the E.F.T.A. Convention was finally signed on November 20,
1959. Essentially, it was the Maudling Free Trade Area writ
small.

In addition to the specific, if limited, economic and trading
advantages which the E.F.T.A. seemed to promise its members,
three main motives appear to have inspired it. The first was
probably to prevent other countries from following the Greek
and Turkish example by seeking a separate peace with the
Common Market and thus crystallizing trade and investment
patterns in the Community's favour. The second was clearly to
strengthen the hand of non-Community members of O.E.E.C. in
pressing the Community for a wider Free Trade Area, partly
by putting competitive pressure on German and Dutch exporters
in the markets of the Outer Seven. The third motive was no
doubt to prove that a free trading arrangement of this sort was
technically feasible—although any analogy between the Outer
Seven and the original Free Trade Area plan was heavily qualified by the smaller size and scattered location of the E.F.T.A.,
as well as by Great Britain's preponderant position within it.
Finally, a fourth effect, if not a motive, of the Outer Seven
arrangement was to underline the so-called "division of Europe"
between the Six and Seven—although here again, as Professor
Hallstein dryly remarked, " 'political divisions' are not automatic
chemical reactions. They can only occur if politicians want them
—and I can't imagine any statesman being willing to take on
such a responsibility".[19] However, it was partly in response to

the co-existence of the Six and Seven that the United States for the first time decided to take an active part in the debate, by attending, with Western European statesmen, a special meeting in Paris in January 1960, from whose deliberations three main consequences derived. First, the O.E.E.C. was re-organized as the O.E.C.D., the Organization for Economic Co-operation and Development; secondly, a new Atlantic body was established within it to co-ordinate development aid; and thirdly, the Contact Committee proposed by the Community was set up in another form under the name of "Committee on Trade Problems". The significance of these measures, which in effect gave each party some degree of satisfaction, was that they broadened the specifically European focus of efforts at economic co-operation by including the United States and Canada as full members instead of just observers in the new O.E.C.D.; they gave greater emphasis to the need to assist developing countries now that Europe was on its feet again; and they postponed further discussion of the wider Free Trade Area by concentrating attention on any practical problems raised by the Common Market for its other European partners. In fact, the Committee on Trade Problems, when it finally got down to business, found that there were very few such problems to solve.

The broader consequences of these moves are still in the process of emerging : but within Europe itself they were chiefly important as the funeral service of the old Free Trade Area. In this respect, it rapidly became clear that the E.F.T.A. had failed in one of its principal objects; and many people were tempted to regard it as a blind alley which had merely delayed and made more difficult any serious settlement between Great Britain and the European Community. On the other hand, the most conclusive way of identifying any blind alley is to explore it; and in retrospect, both the old Free Trade Area and the Outer Seven may be seen to mark a beginning as well as an end. Already the Free Trade Area project betokened, and helped in turn to stimulate, growing British interest in the European Community. By proposing to open Britain's frontiers to the European market, and the European market to her own producers, it helped to pave the way for more radical solutions. In this sense, it may have been more than just another move in the familiar ritual dance. The E.F.T.A., again, intensified not only the hope of a wider Free Trade Area, but also the degree of Britain's practical involvement in many of the problems of economic integration; and the widespread public controversy surrounding all these questions undoubtedly helped to increase general awareness of the issues and their importance, and to render more acceptable the further step that was to come.

For some time, indeed, a number of voices in the British Press, in industry, and elsewhere, had been suggesting that Britain "take the plunge" and join the European Community. Hints that the Government was taking such suggestions seriously culminated on July 31, 1961, in the Prime Minister's announcement to the House of Commons that Britain was to ask for negotiations with the European Economic Community to see if mutually acceptable conditions could be worked out for British membership. On the following day, the Common Market Commission officially and warmly welcomed this decision—as did all the member Governments—and promised to give its full support to a positive solution of the many problems involved. After a preliminary statement to the Ministers of the Community countries in Paris on October 10, the negotiations proper began in Brussels on November 8, 1961.

Many factors no doubt contributed to this momentous decision. Some of them, undoubtedly, were economic. Despite the assurances given by the Common Market that it would seek to remedy any trade difficulties that its establishment might cause, and despite the fact that its imports had continued to rise as its prosperity grew, British industry was far from happy to see its French and German rivals progressively securing duty-free access

to each other's markets while Britain remained outside. Nor was
it any happier about exclusion from the potential benefits of a
large home market, and—despite occasional xenophobic outcries
—from a centre of attraction for increasing quantities of transatlantic capital. With these advantages, European industries
threatened, and indeed began, to become formidable competitors
in world export markets, including certain Commonwealth countries which some British salesmen tended to regard as their own
preserve. If such challenges made some industries in Britain eager
to meet them by entering the Common Market, several economists had recently suggested that less dynamic firms stood in
need, not so much of equal access to the Common Market, as of
direct competition within it in order to stimulate their latent
powers. A more extreme version of this argument was that the
British economy as a whole required the spring-cleaning of a few
bankruptcies among the inefficient: a more primitive variant
was the belief that mere contact with an expanding Community
would somehow infect Great Britain with economic growth. The
former found most support among tub-thumping prophets of "a
showdown with the unions"; and the latter was somewhat invalidated by the unimpressive growth rate of Belgium, already a
member of the Common Market: but while many were properly
wary of such exaggerations, few could resist the feeling that at all
events continued protection within a small but prosperous market
was the reverse of what was needed. There were even suggestions
for unilateral tariff-cutting; and had President Kennedy at that
time made the proposals for drastic world-wide tariff reductions
that he was later to air at the beginning of 1962, it is possible
that some advocates of a wider market for Britain might have
found them an acceptable substitute for entering the Community.
As it was, however, the only alternative seemed to be a thoroughgoing attempt to expand Commonwealth trade: but this encountered not only the difficulty that Commonwealth Preference
margins were already being eroded (partly by slow inflation

which reduced the *ad valorem* incidence of specific duties), but also the reluctance of some Commonwealth countries themselves to open their markets to further industrial imports from Britain at a time when they were painfully developing their own production of manufactures. What was more, despite the importance of the Commonwealth market, it was expanding far more slowly than that of Western Europe, and it was already being invaded by Britain's continental and transatlantic competitors.

Such, in a highly simplified form, was the economic case that was most commonly advanced for British membership of the Common Market during the months of debate in 1961. Some of it, since it rested on forecasts of future development, was bound to be speculative, and the confidence of some of its advocates, for example, might easily be checked—though not, I think, invalidated—by a slowing-down of the European Community's rate of growth. The economic argument, however, was never more than a part—and in my view not the most important part—of the case for British membership. Politics, quite properly, were also very much involved.

The Free Trade Area negotiations had been handled by the Board of Trade. Already, however, in the early weeks of 1960, the Foreign Office had begun to take a hand in the work of such bodies as the Committee on Trade Policy; and for some months before Mr. Macmillan's announcement, senior British diplomats who three years earlier had still been telling me, *à propos* of the Common Market's transition period, "You're very optimistic, Richard, but twelve years is a very long time", were now openly confiding that they thought Britain must join. The Foreign Office, indeed, had long been aware of the political significance of the European Community; and it was an index of Great Britain's serious political intentions that the negotiations for membership should have been placed in Foreign Office hands. One reason, no doubt, was that the political case for Britain's membership had been growing notably stronger as she began to experience some of the setbacks which had earlier convinced her continental neighbours of the need to band together. The Suez *débâcle*, the failure of Blue Streak, the dangerous farce of the Paris Summit meeting, and the Prime Minister's visit to Moscow —all had underlined the *ridimensionamento* referred to earlier. The world was assuredly a world of giants; and Great Britain, although richer and more powerful in absolute terms than at any previous period of her history, was still only one country in a world increasingly organized in continents. Where would she be if on her doorstep there were to arise a politically united Europe? Could the allegiance of the Commonwealth countries compensate her for her comparative loss of stature? Could her special relationship with the United States remain quite so special? And if not, would she not find herself becoming more and more a passive spectator in world politics, essentially always reacting to decisions taken by others? Would not this be a loss of real sovereignty without any compensating advantages? Would it not be better to join in the pooling of sovereignty and thereby preserve and even increase her power?

These, I imagine, were some of the questions that must have been asked in the corridors of Whitehall during the spring and summer of 1961. Essentially, they were relevant whatever the policies that the Community's existing member states seemed likely to follow: indeed, their force was greater on issues where British policy might be likely to disagree with them. Outside the Community, Britain's voice might be respected, but it might fail to persuade: inside, she would be able to exert some influence upon any common action, whether on N.A.T.O., Berlin, Africa, German reunification, trade with the Eastern bloc, or policy *vis-à-vis* developing and low-wage countries. On matters of high foreign policy and defence, it would be well-nigh impossible to over-rule her: and even in fields specifically charted by the Rome Treaty, where the member states were irrevocably committed to economic union, it would still be highly unlikely that her partners would ride rough-shod over her interests, since her continued support would be needed in other fields. If the powers increasingly allotted to the "Eurocrats" of the Commission in Brussels looked daunting to British-trained officials, it was sometimes forgotten that British subjects would figure on its staff—as indeed, in very small numbers, they already do. The Court of Justice, likewise, would also include British nationals; and the same would apply to the European Parliament, which some British M.P.s seemed to fear on account of its "supranational" attributes, although Europeans have always criticized it, more shrewdly, for the limitations so far imposed upon its powers. The European Investment Bank, the European Social Fund, the agricultural fund, the overseas Development Fund—all would be partly British institutions, partly devoted to British ends. In this sense, "Brussels" would no longer stand for something alien, but would rather represent the provisional headquarters of a structure in which Britain was intimately involved. Seen in this perspective, many of the forebodings voiced on grounds of "losing sovereignty" seemed to resemble the pre-nuptial tremors of a confirmed bachelor who had not yet fully accepted the idea that "that woman" might one day become "my wife".

Not all the problems, of course, were political or psychological —although many, like the fear of low-wage competition from the continent or of an influx of foreign labour, proved largely illusory in the light of the facts : fringe benefits financed by employers made overall wage rates on the continent just as attractive as in Great Britain, and the fear of a foreign labour invasion was largely belied, not only by the tightness of the labour market, but also by the Rome Treaty, which provides for free movement of labour only in so far as jobs are actually available. Other problems, such as the harmonization of laws and the mutual recognition of diplomas, were technically highly complex, but by no means insurmountable; while others still, including the crucial questions of economic and monetary policy, were no more difficult for Great Britain than for the existing members of the Community, who found them intractable enough, but nevertheless remained undaunted.

Great Britain's more particular problems, however, were three-fold—or rather, they could be summarized under three comprehensive headings. The first was the adaptation of Britain's subsidized agriculture to a European system based on levies on imports; the second was the safeguarding of essential Commonwealth trading interests while Britain gradually adopted the Community's common external tariff; and the third was the future of her partners in E.F.T.A., of whom Denmark and Norway applied for Community membership, while Austria, Portugal, Sweden, and Switzerland sought some form of association in the hope of achieving "a single European market". The picture was further complicated by a request for membership from the Republic of Ireland, whose application, indeed, was made even before Great Britain's; while in February 1962, even Spain submitted an application for association and eventual possible membership.

All these questions are the subject of negotiation and discussion at the time of writing, and it is impossible to predict at this stage what will emerge. For Great Britain, at first sight, the domestic agricultural problem would seem to be the easiest to solve : but its solution would seem to necessitate a slight increase in home food prices, offset by the removal of subsidies. In so far as British agriculture is competitive with its continental counterparts, this should cause no great upheaval : but special measures seem likely to be necessary in the case of horticulture, and British farmers would no doubt have to acquire a technique for lobbying in Brussels as well as in Whitehall Place.

The problems of the Commonwealth, on the other hand, are generally admitted to be the most difficult, since their settlement would seem to involve a gradual tapering-off of the Commonwealth preference system—although the value of preference is in any case diminishing, and as a member of the Community

Great Britain would be better placed to increase her development aid. Some tropical countries of the Commonwealth, particularly in Africa, might hope for association with the European
Community on lines similar to those of the association of former
French, Belgian, Italian, and Dutch colonies. For some crucial
raw materials and manufactures, a lower or a suspended duty
might perhaps be introduced into the common external tariff.
But the two most intractable of the Commonwealth's problems
are those of its exports of temperate foodstuffs into Great Britain,
which would normally be subject to the Community's external
levy, and of the developing Commonwealth countries' exports
of manufactured products, including textiles from India, Pakis-
tan, and Hong Kong, which would face the common external
tariff. While it is by no means certain that the levy and the
tariff respectively would bring the trade to a standstill, there is
no doubt that the difficulties arising—for instance over New
Zealand dairy products—might well be serious; and in the long
term they raise issues of economic policy which can only be
solved on a world-wide basis by means of international stabilization agreements and far-sighted generosity on the part of
industrialized nations *vis-à-vis* the poorer countries of the world.
In the shorter term, it would no doubt be sufficient to provide
for transitional measures, but it would be necessary to make sure
that these moved in the direction of suitable long-term arrangements, rather than working against them and making their realization even more difficult than it is.

By comparison with these world-wide issues, the problem of
the other European countries is very much simpler : but this too
involves a series of political choices—for all parties—that will
undoubtedly be difficult to make. It is not yet by any means
certain what policy the Community will adopt as regards the
"single European market", which to some of its members seems
to present many of the disadvantages of the Free Trade Area
concept in a slightly different guise. Should countries that are

unwilling or unable to share the Community's political aims be allowed to participate in its commercial benefits to a degree denied, for example, to the United States? Can a neutral country conscientiously sign the Rome Treaty? Can a non-democratic country do so? Can a developing country stand the strain? Should the same treatment be accorded to countries that are neutral by choice, like Switzerland, and those that are forced to be neutral for fear of Russian threats, like Austria? All these queries at present indicate genuine uncertainties: but they also indicate genuine doubts.

Mention of these doubts is a reminder that even in the case of Great Britain, not all the difficulties lay on the British side. Presented with the British application for membership of the Community, its existing members themselves faced a serious problem. On the one hand, the British application was a resounding testimony to the Community's success: but on the other, might it not—perhaps unwittingly—be another move in the ritual dance? Would the entry of Great Britain, bringing with her the problems of the Commonwealth, the responsibilities of the Sterling Area, and all her own traditional attitudes, in fact risk diluting the Community and sapping its ability to move ahead to closer union and common action in other fields? Even those who most warmly welcomed Great Britain were somewhat dismayed by the eagerness with which some British spokesmen and statesmen embraced General de Gaulle's less radical formula of *"l'Europe des Etats"*. Indeed, when a German colleague remarked to me that British membership of the Community was politically *"unvermeidbar"*, the fact that this word, like the French *"inévitable"*, meant both "inevitable" and "unavoidable", was not without significance and piquancy. It says much, therefore, for the goodwill and imagination of continental Europeans—in governments and Community institutions alike—that their welcome to the British request for membership was so immediate and so warm. Jean Monnet and his colleagues, in particular, were convinced that once inside the Community, Great Britain would work loyally to further its aims : they felt, too, that practical experience of life within it would eventually lead her to accept future measures of integration for which the time was not yet ripe. Her continued absence, moreover, had in itself discouraged certain member states of the Community who feared to go too far without her. In integration, they believed, *l'appétit vient en mangeant*.[20]

How long the present negotiations will take, and what precisely will be their outcome, are questions for prophets, not historians or reporters. Nevertheless, some prophecies may be in order, if only to avoid future dismay. The first is that the negotiations will undoubtedly be lengthy. A second is that there will undoubtedly be crises and difficulties. A third is that not everyone will declare himself satisfied with the results. For my own part, I find it hard to believe that this will lead to failure; and I am convinced that if Great Britain enters the Community in the right spirit, she will find that membership is not just a *pis aller*, a case of "if you can't lick 'em, join 'em", or a slightly better alternative to remaining outside, but an immense and positive opportunity to help tackle some of the outstanding problems which concern the world as a whole.

CHAPTER VIII

EUROPE AND THE WIDER WORLD

ALTHOUGH ONE OF the basic reasons for European integration is the rapid and revolutionary changes that have transformed the modern world, and in which growing unity in Europe is itself in turn a factor, only half a dozen of the nearly four hundred pages in the Common Market Treaty's English version are in fact devoted to its foreign affairs. One of the Community's principal tasks in its first four years' existence, therefore, was to develop the main lines of its future policy *vis-à-vis* the rest of the world. Even without Great Britain, the problems it faced were serious: with Great Britain's application for membership, their solution became even more urgent. Some of them may be said to have arisen as a result of the Community's existence. In other cases, its existence merely highlighted problems already of long standing. In general, however, the consolidation of the Community has made both classes of problem easier to solve.

The external problems arising from the Community's existence were essentially of two kinds—those due to its own customs and economic union, and those due to the association with it of the colonies and former colonies of its member states. Controversy over the first began very early in the Common Market's existence, and even before its Treaty had come into effect. Many of its neighbours and trading partners feared that the abolition of its internal trade barriers, coupled with the merging of its members' external tariffs into one single tariff, would be likely to reduce its imports from outside; and although the Community pointed out that its tariff was no more protective than those it would replace,

and therefore remained in conformity with the rules of the
G.A.T.T., the autumn 1957 session of the G.A.T.T. in Geneva
made it clear that not all its members accepted this thesis. In
Europe, meanwhile, the argument most frequently advanced in
favour of the O.E.E.C.-wide Free Trade Area was that the
Community was planning to "discriminate" against its O.E.E.C.
partners, despite the fact that the O.E.E.C.'s rules counten-
anced customs unions, as did the G.A.T.T. In international legal
terms, the Community's case was justified : its common external
tariff was based on an arithmetical average of its members' previous national tariffs, which meant in broad terms that the low
Benelux tariff, surrounding a market of 20 million consumers,
would go up, while the German tariff, surrounding some 50
million, would remain much the same, and the French and
Italian tariffs, surrounding 90 million, would go down. As it
turned out, the average incidence of the common external tariff
was 7.4 per cent—several points below that of the British non-
preferential level, even on manufactured goods.

Purely legal justification, however, failed to satisfy the Community's critics. At the time, all that the Community could
answer was that it would examine and try to solve any real
difficulties that its trading partners might experience : but this
again was not wholly satisfactory, for two main reasons. First,
it could only be a promise until some real difficulties occurred;
and secondly, it was not merely the maintenance of their trade
with the Community that its partners had in mind : what they
sought was an increase of their outlets in the Community at the
same rate as the expansion of intra-Community trade. In the
event, during the first four years, the Community's overall imports
actually increased, but not as fast as trade within it. Nevertheless,
it did make special efforts to take account of the fears which had
been expressed. As has been seen already, after the failure of the
Free Trade Area negotiations, it agreed to extend—first to its
neighbours in the O.E.E.C., and in the second case to its partners

in the G.A.T.T.—some of the first mutual trade concessions that its members made on the way to the full Common Market. Then, when its own growing momentum encouraged it to accelerate the realisation of the Common Market and therefore its moves towards the common external tariff, the Community provisionally lowered the latter by 20 per cent, in anticipation of the negotiations then about to begin in the G.A.T.T. on the proposal of Mr. C. Douglas Dillon. At the time of writing, these negotiations were on the point of completion; and they seemed likely to be followed by further moves, both as a result of the Community's expressed willingness to continue in a liberal direction and in implementation of the tariff-cutting proposals made in January 1962 by President Kennedy.[1]

If the common external tariff was one source of worry for the Community's trading partners, another was the association with it of the so-called "overseas countries and territories"—the colonies and former colonies of its member states, mostly producers of tropical or sub-tropical products such as coffee, cocoa, bananas, palm oil, and so on. In the G.A.T.T. the Community argued that the association was legally justified, since it took the form of a free trade area, not a preference zone : but this defence was qualified by the fact that the overseas associates were entitled to maintain revenue duties in their trade with the Community, as well as protective duties to shelter any infant industries. Moreover, it failed to meet the argument that other tropical producers were hoping to develop their outlets in Europe. Here once again the Community replied that the expansion of the Community market would also benefit other countries, and in the first four years of its existence, the facts were largely to bear this out. Nevertheless, the situation remained unsatisfactory for several reasons. Non-associated countries continued to resent the privileges enjoyed by the associates, while the latter found that the preference they enjoyed in the Community market was far less influential in securing them satisfactory outlets than the various long-term sales guarantees still granted them by their former mother countries, and in particular by France. What was more, since the conclusion of the Rome Treaty and of the Association itself, many of the African countries had become independent; and this development, together with the expiry at the end of 1962 of the financing Convention dealing with the overseas Development Fund, seemed to provide an opportunity to revise the whole Association, in conjunction with those overseas states that elected to do so, in order both to improve the position for the associates themselves and to reduce the element of discrimination against other countries. Re-negotiations to this end, with 16 independent African and Madagascar states, were in progress at the time of writing : they had as their basis a series of proposals from the Common Market Commission which envisaged a lowering of the external tariff on certain tropical products, coupled with an increase of aid and measures to stabilize market outlets and prices. Somewhat similar ideas were mooted by Great Britain for the possible association of various Commonwealth countries, again chiefly in Africa : but the reactions of the world's remaining tropical producers were still uncertain.

Meanwhile, various non-member countries outside Europe had already approached the Community with a view to securing special treatment for their exports. During 1960, in particular, a number of Latin American countries submitted memoranda expressing their concerns, especially over coffee and banana exports; and the Community agreed to joint consultation on these subjects. Japan, likewise, showed increasing interest in securing bilateral talks; and so, it was reported, did Israel. In dealing with these suppliants, the Community suffered from the same handicaps as it had encountered during the Free Trade Area negotiations in Europe : first, that it had not yet fully worked out its own foreign trade policy, and secondly that any special concessions it granted ran the risk of aggravating the difficulties of third parties. Indeed, as the number of suppliants

increased, it became more and more apparent that special concessions granted to almost everyone would be merely a complicated and discriminatory form of general, world-wide agreement,
for which the proper international and multilateral negotiating
forum was the G.A.T.T.

The apprehensions provoked by the common external tariff
and by the association of overseas states, however, were only
some of the problems which faced the Community in its dealings
with the rest of the world. Even they were partly something for
which the Community itself was not wholly responsible : for the
former was in part the problem of trade liberalization in general,
and the latter was deeply involved with the world-wide questions
of aid to developing countries—including that of outlets for their
manufactures—and the stabilization of basic commodity markets.
If in this way the creation of the Community merely helped to
spotlight existing economic issues, the same applied to some of
the other questions that still vex it—the problems of world agriculture, of world liquidity, of the overall balance of payments,
and of ways to avoid excessive fluctuations in the business cycle.[2]

These problems are too familiar to require re-statement : but
what is worth emphasizing is that the creation of the European
Community, while it makes them more obvious, also provides a
greater opportunity for solving them. The basic reason is the
concentration of effort that the Community itself involves—not
only because a larger market may in itself become a stabilizing
factor, but also because world-wide solutions are easier to achieve
if several states, representing a large economic unit, have already
had to face the problem on a smaller scale, and have already
been obliged to work out a joint approach to its wider ramifications. To make the Common Market work, for instance, monetary policy must be co-ordinated : but this is virtually impossible
without action on a wider scale. To achieve a common agricultural policy, again, the Community is obliged to take into account
the world-wide problems of balancing supply and demand. With

the negotiation for British entry to the Community, such considerations acquired an added force : for if the problems of Commonwealth countries were to be settled satisfactorily, this could only be achieved in the longer term by means of worldwide agreements on a non-discriminatory basis, involving a reform and a spring-cleaning of the whole international economic scene.

It is against such a background, finally, that the Community's relations with the United States need to be considered. Politically, the United States had always supported the postwar moves towards true European unity—not only to ensure that Western Europe could once more stand on its own feet economically, but also in the hope that unity would give it the political strength and stability to resist—to take one example—the temptations of a second Rapallo.

Economically, the United States' attitude remained equally clear : any discrimination against American trade caused by the fact of the Common Market should be offset by these political advantages, and such discrimination should be as small as was compatible with the achievement of real unity. Washington was understandably lukewarm over plans for commercial discrimination, whether by the Free Trade Area or by purely commercial association with the Community, if they seemed to lack political content; and more recently there began to be still more insistence upon liberal policies which would reduce any discriminatory effect.[3] This tendency became more marked in 1960, with the deterioration of the United States' balance of payments, and in 1961, when the Community was engaged in trying to work out its own common agricultural policy, necessarily involving a degree of protection from world markets, but looking ahead nevertheless to the longer-term settlement of world agricultural problems by international agreement. The prospect of British membership of the Community, moreover, gave an added urgency to U.S. economic concern. Already, the United States had helped to transform the purely European O.E.E.C. into the O.E.C.D. : in the new title, the word "European" was dropped, and the word "Development" added—a double sign that the United States favoured a world-wide rather than a wider European approach to economic co-operation, and that it expected the nations of Europe to help it more fully in bearing the burden of aid to developing countries. Clearly, what was slowly evolving was economic interdependence across the Atlantic; and this led to much talk of the prospects for an "Atlantic Community", or an "open partnership", as this somewhat loose concept was better described by President Kennedy in the Message to Congress early in 1962 whereby he requested special tariff powers to negotiate with the European Community.

At the time of writing, it was obviously too early to comment in detail on the likely outcome of President Kennedy's proposals.[4] In one sense, what he requested was merely the right to do something of what most other members of the G.A.T.T. were empowered to do already—that is, to negotiate tariff cuts without having his hands unduly tied by the legislature, with an arbitrary limit to the degree of tariff reduction, a series of "peril points" on certain products which restricted even this limit, and a lapsing of even these meagre powers after a certain time. This was the most that the former Trade Agreements Act permitted : but the new proposals would empower the President to negotiate the U.S. tariff down to zero on goods in which the Community and the U.S. do 80 per cent of world trade, as well as on some tropical products, and down to 50 per cent of the previous level on most other items. Certain goods, however, would still be subject to special Congressional scrutiny, and in some cases the tariff could be unilaterally raised even after the negotiation. At the same time, special aid measures could be extended to help U.S. industry to adjust to the new situation.

These proposals clearly marked a further break with lingering traditions of the old isolationism and protectionism which the

U.S. government had abandoned with World War II, and if successful they should certainly enable both the United States and the European Community to pursue the liberal policies they profess. They were also a clear recognition by the United States of the success and the importance of European economic integration; and they revealed, I think, a realization that with Great Britain once inside the Community the United States would face just such a problem of *ridimensionamento* as Great Britain found herself facing when the Community came into being. What was equally clear, however, was that such proposals could only be a beginning. Were tariffs to be cut to zero only on products which chiefly interested the United States and the European Community, this would in fact discriminate against countries whose interests lay elsewhere, even if the extension to them of these tariff cuts, under the most-favoured-nation rules of the G.A.T.T., were legally speaking to have removed the element of discrimination. Were certain products even in this range to be excepted from tariff-cutting, or to be subject to higher tariffs later on, this might unduly clog the negotiation and destroy confidence elsewhere. Furthermore, as has already been suggested in discussion of economic integration, the simple cutting of tariffs would be pointless, beyond a certain degree of liberalization, if the underlying reasons for the tariffs were to remain untouched, and if tariff protection were merely to be replaced, for example, by subsidies on the one hand and anti-dumping measures on the other. In fact, even the elimination of all forms of protection on an Atlantic basis would be merely a partial reform of the world's economy if it were not supplemented, perhaps in the O.E.C.D., by measures of economic co-operation in some of the fields already mentioned, and perhaps eventually by the establishment of institutions of greater strength on a wider international plane. *C'est le premier pas qui coûte*, no doubt : but in all such matters also, *c'est le dernier pas qui compte*. Perhaps it will be Europe's task to lead the way.

CHAPTER IX

THE WAY AHEAD

Books on contemporary subjects customarily conclude with a chapter under some such title as the above. In the case of the European Community, it is particularly appropriate—and particularly difficult: for everything that has been said hitherto should suggest two main conclusions. First, that the Common Market Treaty is not the last volume in a trilogy, but merely a further instalment of a story that began long before this particular volume was conceived, and one that will continue into further chapters as yet unwritten, which may embrace an even wider field. Secondly, that the European Community is already an evolving entity, capable of adapting itself to new situations, new demands, and new emphases. It is broad enough to accommodate the liberal and the *dirigiste*, the Christian Democrat and the Socialist, the federalist and the confederalist, the large-scale nation-state and the tiny Grand Duchy. It has already survived some crises: it has moved successfully into the second stage of the Common Market: with any luck, it will be able to enlist new recruits. Certainly, it needs further strengthening—perhaps by means of some political union of states, but more essentially, to my mind, by merging its three Executives into one High Commission, as the Netherlands has proposed, and by perhaps electing the European Parliament by direct universal suffrage, according to the Parliament's own project. Certainly, too, the full application of the Rome Treaties, and especially of the Common Market Treaty, will require the preparation of many more detailed rules than the Treaties themselves contain. Above all, it will require a continuing political will on the part of its peoples and member governments; and the plan for new forms of political union, even if only confederal, may possibly help it to this end. Whether, one day, the new methods of political organization between states that the Community has pioneered may lead to some wider union of peoples, perhaps to realize that dream of perpetual world peace that inspired so many plans for European unity, is a darker, more distant question. What is already certain, however, is that the European Community is a continuous creation. There need be no resting-place for the European idea.

NOTES

CHAPTER I

[1] For a cautious discussion of this question, see Alexander Lamfalussy, "Europe's Progress: Due to Common Market?", *Lloyds Bank Review*, New Series, No. 62, October 1961, pp. 1–16.

[2] For details, see information published by *Opera Mundi Europe*, by *Europe* News Agency, and by the *Britain in Europe Newsletter*, among other usually reliable sources.

[3] "The Eurocrats", *Economist*, Vol. CC, No. 6153 (July 29, 1961), p. 449.

[4] "Then Will It Live . . ." (Cover story on Jean Monnet), *Time*, Atlantic Edition, Vol. LXXVIII, No. 14 (October 6, 1961), p. 20.

CHAPTER II

[1] Walter Ullmann, *The Growth of Papal Government in the Middle Ages* (London, 1955), p. 106.

[2] William of Malmesbury, *Gesta Regum* (ed. W. Stubbs), Rolls Series, 2 vols. (London, 1887–9), Vol. II, p. 395, quoted by Denys Hay, *Europe: the Emergence of an Idea* (Edinburgh, 1957), pp. 30 ff., to which much of this chapter is indebted. Since William's account was written thirty years after Clermont, it may be more symptomatic of his than of Urban's attitude. For Gregory VII, see Hay, *op. cit.*, p. 52. On the 1054 "schism", cf. my own article, "East and West in 1054", *Cambridge Historical Journal*, vol. xi, no. 2 (1954), pp. 133–148.

[3] Dante, *De Monarchia*, Book III, chap. xiv; Hay, *op. cit.*, pp. 58–60.

[4] H. Bonet, *Somnium super materia scismatis*, in *l'Apparicion maistre Jehan de Meun* (ed. I. Arnold), Paris, 1926, p. 106; Hay, *op. cit.*, p. 76.

[5] Hay, *op. cit.*, p. 85.

[6] In the Basle reprint of Sebastian Münster's *Cosmographia Universalis*, f. xli; Hay, *op. cit.*, p. 119 and frontispiece.

[7] *Purchas His Pilgrimes* (Hakluyt Society, Extra Series), Vol. I (1905), pp. 248 ff.; Hay *op. cit.*, pp. 120 ff.

[8] Hay, *op. cit.*, p. 117.

[9] Cf. Bernard Voyenne, *Petite histoire de l'idée européene*, 2nd. ed. (Paris, 1954), pp. 52 ff.

[10] F. le Van Baumer, "The Church of England and the common corps of Christendom", *Journal of Modern History*, Vol. XVI (1944), p. 7; Hay, *op. cit.*, p. 112.

[11] "Discours des choses prédites par le Roi Henri le Grand", *Notices et*

documents publés par la Societé de l'Histoire de France (Paris, 1884), p. 406; Voyenne, *op. cit.,* p. 77.

[12] Letter to Mme de Brinon, September 29, 1691; Voyenne, *op. cit.,* p. 90.

[13] David Thomson, *Europe Since Napoleon* (London, 1957), p. 601.

[14] *Letters on the Regicide Peace,* I, iii, in *Select Works,* Vol. III (Oxford, 1878), p. 80.

[15] Voyenne, *op. cit.,* pp. 139–40.

[16] Voyenne, *op. cit.,* p. 100.

[17] Voyenne, *op. cit.,* pp. 102–8.

[18] Voyenne, *op. cit.,* pp. 104, 114.

[19] Thomson, *op. cit.,* p. 76.

[20] Voyenne, *op. cit.,* 121–6.

[21] *Du principe fédératif,* ed. Charles-Brun, pp. 155–6; Voyenne, *op. cit.,* p. 137.

[22] Voyenne, *op. cit.,* pp. 144–5.

[23] Voyenne, *op. cit.,* p. 159.

[24] Henry J. Forman, *Grecian Italy* (London, 1927), p. 29.

[25] Rilke and Gide, *Correspondence 1909–1926* (Paris, 1952), pp. 170, 182–3, 189, 224.

[26] Uwe Kitzinger, *The Challenge of the Common Market* (Oxford, 1961), p. 2.

[27] R. Colin Beever, *European Unity and the Trade Union Movements* (Leyden, 1961), p. 283.

CHAPTER III

[1] *History of the Public Revenue of the British Empire* (1785–1790), ii, 105; W. Cunningham, *The Growth of English Industry and Commerce in Modern Times,* 6th ed. (Cambridge, 1921), ii, p. 867.

[2] *The National System of Political Economy* (Transl. S.S. Lloyd), p. 93; Alexander Gray, *The Development of Economic Doctrine* (London, 1931), pp. 234–5; E. Roll, *A History of Economic Thought* (revised, London, 1961), pp. 227–31.

[3] *Op. cit.,* ii, p. 870.

[4] A. J. Grant and Harold Temperley, *Europe in the Nineteenth and Twentieth Centuries* (4th ed., London, 1932), p. 404. In fact, the total population of the new colonial territories was over 120 million.

[5] Thomson, *op. cit.,* pp. 473–4.

[6] London and New York, 1920.

[7] *The Second World War,* Vol. I, *The Gathering Storm* (London, Penguin edition, 1960), p. 24.

[8] *Op. cit.,* p. 36.

[9] Rolf Sannwald & Jacques Stohler, *Wirtschaftliche Integration: Theoretische Voraussetzungen und Folgen eines Europäischen Zusammenschlusses* (Basel/Tübingen, 1958), p. 1. Statistics quoted above are from various sources, including this study, pp. 1–7, and Jacques Trempont, *L'Unification de l'Europe,* (Amiens/Bruxelles, 1955), pp. 20–28.

[10] *The Wealth of Nations,* Book I, title of chapter iii (Everyman's Library edition, London, 1910), Vol. I, p. 15.

11 J. Frederic Dewhurst, John O. Coppock, P. Lamartine Yates and associates, *Europe's Needs and Resources* (New York, 1961), pp. 404–7, 439.

12 *Mitteleuropa*, p. 249, quoted by E. Strauss, *Common Sense About the Common Market* (London, 1958), p. 31.

13 W. O. Henderson, *The Zollverein* (1939), p. 343; Strauss, *op cit.,* p. 17.

14 *Customs Unions: A League of Nations Contribution to the Study of Customs Union Problems* (New York, 1947), p. 74. On customs unions, cf. also Jacob Viner, *The Customs Union Issue* (New York, 1951), James E. Meade, *Problems of Economic Union* (London, 1953) and *The Theory of Customs Unions* (Amsterdam, 1956).

15 J.-F. Deniau, *The Common Market* (London, 1960), p. 20.

CHAPTER IV

1 Charles de Gaulle, *Mémoires de Guerre,* Vol. III, *Le Salut*, pp. 57–58. On "strategic and economic federation", *ibid.,* Vol II, *L'Unité*, p. 481 (letter to René Massigli, February 24, 1944); on Pius XII, *ibid.,* Vol. II, p. 287. (All quotations from *Livre de poche* edition, Paris, 1959–61.) On René Mayer, cf. Roger Massip, *Voici L'Europe* (Paris, 1958), p. 89. Cf. also Arnold J. Zurcher, *The Struggle to Unite Europe* (New York, 1958), pp. v, 10–18, 19; and C. Grove Haines (ed.) *European Integration* (Baltimore, 1957), p. 50. Cf. also George Orwell, "Towards European Unity", *Partisan Review,* July–August 1947.

2 Chester Wilmot, *The Struggle for Europe* (London, 1952); Fontana Books edition (1959), p. 722.

3 But not to be confused with the Bank for International Settlements (B.I.S.), set up in 1930 to promote co-operation between central banks and to act as trustee or agent for international financial settlements.

4 George Marshall, speech at Harvard, June 5, 1947.

5 Miriam Camps, *The European Common Market and American Policy* (Princeton, 1956), p. 2.

6 Cf. Max Beloff, *New Dimensions in Foreign Policy* (London, 1961), p. 38.

7 Economic Co-operation Act of April 3, 1948, Section 102 a.

8 Political and Economic Planning (P.E.P.), *European Organisations* (London, 1959), p. 52; Richard Bailey, *L'Intégration économique en Europe* (Turin, 1960), p. 3.

9 P.E.P. *op. cit.,* p. 54.

10 P.E.P., *op. cit.,* p. 75.

11 Robert Marjolin, "Coopération intergouvernementale et autorités supranationales", *Revue Economique,* Vol IX, No. 2 (Paris, March 1958), pp. 267–77; p. 269.

12 R. S. Churchill (ed.), *The Sinews of Peace: Postwar Speeches by Winston S. Churchill* (London, 1948), p. 199.

13 Richard N. Coudenhove-Kalergi, *Die Europäische Nation* (Stuttgart, 1953), p. 120; Zurcher, *op. cit.,* pp. 18, 20.

[14] *Méthodes et mouvements pour unir l'Europe* (*Bulletin du Centre Européen de la Culture*, 6th Year, no. 2, Geneva, May, 1958); Massip, *op. cit.*, pp. 175–6; Zurcher, *op. cit.*, pp. 21–2.

[15] Council of Europe, Directorate of Information, *The First Five Years* (Strasbourg, 1954), p. 23; Zurcher, *op. cit.*, pp. 48–9.

[16] American Committee on United Europe, *United Europe: A Statement of Progress* (New York, 1950), p. 22. On the Philip-Reynaud motion, C. C. Walton, "The Fate of Neo-Federalism in Western Europe," *Western Political Quarterly*, Vol. V, no. 3 (September, 1952), p. 379; Zurcher, *op. cit.*, pp. 50–2. For other proposals, Marinus van der Goes van Naters, *Le développement de l'intégration économique de l'Europe, Première section: Analyse des documents, 2ième édition* (Luxembourg, Assemblée Commune de la C.E.C.A., July, 1955), pp. 14, 20–1.

[17] *La Documentation Française, Série internationale, cccxix, L'Organisation de l'Europe occidentale, Iière partie* (Paris, Présidence du Conseil, July 18, 1955), pp. 17–8; Lord Strang, *At Home and Abroad* (London, 1956), p. 290; Beloff, *op. cit.*, p. 79.

[18] *Report on the institutional reform of the Council of Europe presented by the Bureau of the Assembly*, Rapporteur: M. Pierre-Henri Teitgen, December 20, 1957, Assembly Document 763; P.E.P., *op. cit.*, p. 131. Paul Reynaud, *Unite or Perish*, p. 199, cit. Zurcher, *op. cit.*, p. 55.

CHAPTER V

[1] For the circumstances of the Schuman Declaration, cf. François Fontaine, *La nation frein* (Paris, 1956), pp. 99–101; Massip, *op. cit.*, pp. 9–13; David Schoenbrun, *As France Goes* (London, 1957), pp. 298–301; Pierre Gerbet, "La Genèse du Plan Schuman", *Revue française de science politique* (Paris, 1956), Vol. VI, no. 3, pp. 525–553.

[2] These and later quotations are taken in what I hope is a more logical order from the Schuman Declaration and its preamble. To preserve the flavour of the original, I have sometimes disregarded the rather freer translation made by the E.C.S.C. High Authority.

[3] J. M. Keynes, *The Economic Consequences of the Peace* (New York, 1920) pp. 100–101; William Diebold, Jr., *The Schuman Plan* (New York, 1959), p. 25.

[4] Typescript of a talk given privately in New York, March 16, 1925, and quoted by Diebold, *op. cit.*, p. 27.

[5] Gerbet, *op. cit.*, p. 548; Massip, *op. cit.*, p. 88.

[6] In a lecture given in 1953 at the College of Europe in Bruges.

[7] Fritz Stern, "Adenauer and a Crisis in Weimar Democracy", *Political Science Quarterly* (March 1958), p. 22, n. 55; Diebold, *op. cit.*, pp. 25–6.

[8] Private information; cf. Diebold, *op. cit.*, p. 110; Pierre-Olivier Lapie, *Les trois communautés* (Paris, 1960), p. 44.

[9] Five of the original nine—Spierenburg (now Vice-President), Coppé, Wehrer, Potthoff, and Finet (President from January 1958 to September 1959)—are still members. The President is now Piero Malvestiti, the Italian Christian Democrat and former Minister who was Vice-President

of the Common Market Commission from January 1958 to September 1959. The other new members are Roger Reynaud, a French economist and Christian trade-unionist; Pierre-Olivier Lapie, a former French Minister and Socialist Deputy; and Fritz Hellwig, from the Saar, an economist and former Christian-Democrat Deputy.

[10] High-quality steels whose price, being higher, is relatively less affected by transport costs which in other cases cushion the impact of new competition when trade barriers fall.

[11] Diebold, *op. cit.*, pp. 350–378; cf, also *Rapport fait au nom de la commission du marché commun sur les concentrations d'entreprises dans la Communauté, par M. Henri Fayat* (Common Assembly Document No. 26, Luxembourg, 1956-7). The *"commission"* here is the Assembly's standing committee on the coal and steel market, not the Executive of the European Economic Community.

[12] Jean Monnet, *Les Etats-Unis d'Europe ont commencé* (Paris, 1955), p. 44 (Speech before the first joint meeting of members of the E.C.S.C. Common Assembly and of the Consultative Assembly of the Council of Europe, Strasbourg, June 22, 1953).

[13] *Débats de l'Assemblée Commune*, 2e année no. 1 (Luxembourg, 1953), p. 21.

[14] Pierre Mathijsen, *Le Droit de la Communauté Européene du Charbon et de l'Acier* (The Hague, 1958), pp. 144 ff.; Walter Hallstein, *Address to the 49th Congress of the International Law Association*, Hamburg, August 8, 1960 (E.E.C. Commission, Brussels, stencilled document no. x/4201/1/60-E), pp. 5 ff. Ernst B. Haas, *The Uniting of Europe* (London, 1958) is an interesting and exhaustive attempt to analyse the E.C.S.C. on a federal model; one of Professor Haas's pupils, Leon Lindberg, is working on a similar analysis of Euratom and the Common Market.

[15] Speech before the second session of the Common Assembly, June 15, 1953, *Débats de l'Assemblée Commune*, no. 4 (Luxembourg, 1953), p. 19.

[16] van der Goes van Naters, *op. cit.*, pp. 24–33; Trempont, *op. cit.*, pp. 265–278; *Documentation Française, Série internationale cccxx, L'Organisation de l'Europe occidentale, 2ième partie* (Paris, Présidence du Conseil, July 19, 1955), pp. 42–45.

[17] Charles Janson, Rapporteur to a Chatham House Study Group on *Britain in Western Europe* (Royal Institute of International Affairs, London, 1956), p. 25.

[18] Arthur Koestler, *The Trail of the Dinosaur* (London, 1955), pp. 204–214.

[19] September 12, 1952; *Débats de l'Assemblée Commune*, 2e année no. 1 (Luxembourg, 1953), p. 49.

[20] *Ibid.*, p. 101 (September 13, 1952).

[21] Zurcher, *op. cit.*, p. 108.

[22] "Castellammare and E.D.C.", *New Statesman*, April 17, 1954. For colourful accounts of the Montesi case, see Wayland Young, *The Montesi Scandal* and Melton S. Davis, *All Rome Trembled* (London, 1957).

[23] "Le Rouge et le Noir", *New Statesman*, June 26, 1954.

24 Daniel Lerner & Raymond Aron (ed.), *France Defeats E.D.C.* (New York, 1957), p. 17.

25 *The New York Times*, December 15, 1953.

CHAPTER VI

1 He used substantially the same words when speaking to the High Authority on November 9, 1954, to the Press on November 11, and to the Common Assembly on November 30. (*Débats de l'Assemblée Commune*, no. 7 (Luxembourg, 1955), p. 21.

2 *Comité intergouvernemental créé par la Conférence de Messine, Rapport des Chefs de Délégation aux Ministres des Affaires Etrangères* (Brussels, 1956). The Heads of Delegation were Ludovico Benvenuti (Italy), Félix Gaillard (France), Carl Friedrich Ophuels (Germany), Lambert Schaus (Luxembourg), Baron Jean-Charles Snoy et d'Oppuers (Belgium), and Gerard Marius Verrijn Stuart (Netherlands). Political and Economic Planning published a summarized translation of Part I of the Spaak Report in *Planning*, No. 405, (December 1956).

3 Maurice Faure now headed the French delegation and Johannes Linthorst-Homan that of the Netherlands.

4 "Europe Must Choose: Unity the Key to Better East-West Relations", *The Times* (London), June 16, 1955.

5 "The Growth of the European Movement since World War II", in Haines, *op cit.*, pp. 37–63 (p. 62).

6 Speech to the Consultative Assembly of the Council of Europe, October 21, 1955.

7 Cf. a speech by Albert Coppé, Vice-President of the High Authority, on April 20, 1955, at the National Press Club, Washington, D.C.

8 Action Committee Resolution, September 20, 1956.

9 *Some Aspects of the European Energy Problem* (May, 1955).

10 *A Target for Euratom* (May, 1957).

11 Interview in the *Forum Memo to Members* published by the Atomic Industrial Forum, Inc., Vol. V, no. 6 (New York, June 1958), pp. 14–17 (p. 15).

12 Speech before the European Parliament, December 20, 1961 (Doc. EUR/C/4331/61f, Euratom Commission).

13 Camps, *op. cit.*, p. 3.

14 van der Goes van Naters, *op. cit.*, pp. 16–18, 33–4, 42 ff.

15 High Authority, Economics Division, Doc. no. 5579/55e.

16 "La Communauté Economique Européenne", lecture delivered privately in Luxembourg (High Authority Doc. no. 2725/57/1f), p. 2.

17 May 11, 1956; *Débats de l'Assemblée Commune*, no. 13 (Luxembourg 1956), pp. 482 ff.

18 When Piero Malvestiti left the Commission in September 1959 to assume the Presidency of the High Authority he was replaced by Giuseppe Caron, the Italian former Minister and an active "European". Robert Lemaignen retired in December 1961, to be replaced by Henri Rochereau, former French Minister of Agriculture. Giuseppe Petrilli was replaced in

February 1961 by Lionello Levi Sandri, the Italian Social Democrat, lawyer, senior official, and *Conseiller d'Etat*. Michel Rasquin, who died in April 1958, was replaced by Lambert Schaus, the former Luxembourg Minister who had headed his country's delegation negotiating the Rome Treaties.

19 At their January 1958 meeting, the Foreign Ministers had appointed a German President of the Common Market Commission, a French President of the Euratom Commission, and a Belgian (Paul Finet) President of the High Authority: Italy, as the third largest member country, felt that an Italian should have some equivalent honour. "The Assembly" is the title given that body in the Rome Treaty. On March 19, 1958, it adopted the names *Assemblée parlementaire européenne, Assemblea Parlamentare Europea, Europäisches Parlament,* and *Europese Parlament*. In March 1962 the Parliament changed its French and Italian titles to *Parlement européen and Parlamento Europeo*—in English, "European Parliament".

20 "Economic integration and political unity in Europe", a speech delivered at Harvard University on May 22, 1961, and republished by the London office of the European Community Information Service as no. 2 in its series *Community Topics*.

CHAPTER VII

1 Titles from the Great Seals and Papal correspondence; on 1394, cf. H. F. Hutchinson, *The Hollow Crown: a Life of Richard II* (London, 1961), p. 138.

2 W. S. McKechnie (ed.) *Magna Carta,* 2nd edition (Glasgow, 1915), 485–6.

3 Voltaire, *Lettres philosophiques*, ed. H. Labroue (Paris, 1938), p. 99.

4 A. V. Dicey, *Introduction to the Study of the Law of the Constitution,* 9th edition (London, 1939), p. 179.

5 Prince Bülow's *Diary,* 1899, quoted by Sir Harold Nicolson, *Diplomacy,* 2nd edition (Oxford, 1950), p. 140. On "British is Best", cf. J. H. Huizinga, *Confessions of a European in England* (London, 1958), pp. 78–92.

6 Mary Buchanan, *The Children's Village* (London, 1954).

7 *Trades Union Congress Annual Report, 1947,* p. 420.

8 Count Mensdorff, quoted by Nicolson, *op. cit.,* p. 141.

9 Gilles Anouil, *La Grande-Bretagne et la Communauté Européenne du Charbon et de l'Acier* (Doctoral thesis privately printed, Issoudun, 1960), pp. 87 ff.; Hans Joachim Heiser, *British Policy with regard to the Unification Efforts on the European Continent* (Leyden, 1959), pp. 40–1. Leslie Hunter, *The Road to Brighton Pier* (London, 1959), p. 13, suggests that Bevin and Herbert Morrison together sought ways of avoiding acceptance.

10 Council of Europe, Assembly, *Official Report,* 3rd Session, 1950, p. 514; Anthony Nutting, *Europe Will Not Wait* (London, 1960), pp. 40–1.

11 Nutting, *op. cit.,* pp. 42–6. In 1957, Great Britain launched a similar scheme—the so-called "Grand Design"—to make the Council of Europe's

Consultative Assembly the parent body for the future European Parliament as well as for the existing Assembly of W.E.U.

[12] *Negotiations for a European Free Trade Area*, Cmnd. 641 (H.M.S.O., London, December 1959), p. 8.

[13] Interview with Steven Hamilton, of Radio Nederland's International Service, recorded in Luxembourg, January 14, 1958. Extracts from this were reprinted in *Bulletin from the European Community for Coal and Steel*, Vol. V., no. 2 (London, February 1958).

[14] Cmnd. 641, p. 49. This decision stressed the need for "taking fully into consideration the objectives of the European Economic Community" and affirmed that the F.T.A. "would in practice take effect parallel with the Treaty of Rome"—thereby avoiding a straight declaration that the two must be simultaneous.

[15] Cf. *The Financial Times*, November 15, 1958.

[16] November 18, 1958.

[17] *First* and *Second Memoranda from the Commission of the European Economic Community* (Brussels, February 26, 1959 and September 22, 1959) and Decisions of the E.E.C. Council of November 24, 1959 and May 12, 1960.

[18] The Greek agreement was finally concluded on July 9, 1961.

[19] "Britain and the European Community", interview published in the *Bulletin from the European Community*, Vol. III, no. 1 (London, January 1960).

[20] For a representative view, cf. Pierre Uri, "La Grande-Bretagne rejoint l'Europe", *Le Monde*, 18–20 January 1962.

CHAPTER VIII

[1] On the Community's conformity with the rules of the G.A.T.T. cf. James Jay Allen, *The European Common Market and the G.A.T.T.* (Washington, 1960). The incidence of its tariff is now 5.7 per cent.

[2] For an interesting treatment of this theme, cf. Walter Hallstein, "The European Community and Atlantic Partnership", speech before the National Industrial Conference Board, New York, May 18, 1961.

[3] For the development of U.S. attitudes, cf. particularly the successive reports of Congressional Committees such as the following: *United States Foreign Policy: Worldwide and Domestic Economic Problems and Their Impact on the Foreign Policy of the United States* (No. 44198, August, 1959); *United States Foreign Policy: Western Europe* (No. 46478, October 15, 1959); Edgar M. Bernstein, *International Effects of U.S. Economic Policy* (No. 49762, January 25, 1960); *The United States and World Trade* (No. 65126, March 14, 1961); *A New Look at Foreign Economic Policy* (No. 763720, 1961); *The Task for 1962: a Free World Community* (No. 76490, 1961); *The European Economic Community and the United States* (No. 76810, 1961); *United States Commercial Policy* (No. 77115, 1961); *Trade Restraints in the Western Community* (No. 77172, 1961); *Foreign Economic Policy for the 1960's* (No. 78532, 1962).

[4] The Trade Expansion Act embodying President Kennedy's proposals was approved by Congress on October 4, 1962.

FOR FURTHER REFERENCE

REFERENCES FOR POINTS of detail in the text are given in the notes. What follows is a short list for further reading, mainly in English, selected from the forbidding mass of documentation in various languages that a full bibliography on European integration would be obliged to include.

BIBLIOGRAPHIES

European Community Information Service. *Publications des Communautés Européennes*. Brussels/Luxembourg, January, 1961.

European Community Information Service, London Office. *A Guide to the Study of the European Communities*. Community Topics No. 3, London, 1961.

European Community Information Service, Washington Office. *A Selected Bibliography on European Integration*. Washington, March, 1961.

European Parliament, Directeur de la Documentation Parlementaire et de l'Information. *Bibliographie méthodique trimestrielle*. Luxembourg, quarterly.

Services des Publications des Communautés Européennes. *Publications de le C.E.E.* Brussels, annual.

Wild, J. E. *The European Common Market and the Free Trade Association*. Library Association Special Subject List No. 35. London, 1961.

GENERAL

Allais, Maurice. *L'Europe unie, route de la prosperité*. Paris, 1960.

American Society of International Law. "Regionalism and International Law." *Proceedings of the American Society of International Law*. Washington, 1960, pp. 153–94.

Anderson, Nels. "Opinion on Europe." *European Yearbook*, Vol. V (1959), pp. 143–59.

Ball, M. Margaret. *Nato and the European Union Movement*. New York, 1959.

Beever, R. Colin. *European Unity and the Trade Union Movements*. Leyden, 1961.

Beloff, Max. *Europe and the Europeans: an International Discussion*. London, 1957.
——. "Federalism as a model for international integration." *Yearbook of World Affairs*, Vol. XIII (1959), pp. 188–204.
Bowie, Robert R. and Friedrich, Carl J. (eds.). *Studies in Federalism*. Boston, 1954.
Brann, Benedict. "The Rationalisation of European Institutions." *Cahiers de Bruges*, 1958, No. 1, pp. 17–22.
British Society for International Understanding. *European Unity*. (British Survey No. 196). London, 1960.
Brugmans, Henri. *Les origines de la civilisation européenne*. Liége, 1958.
Committee for Economic Development. "Maximum Challenge." *Saturday Review*, Vol. XLIII, No. 3 (January 16, 1960), pp. 19–48.
Corbett, J. P. *Europe and the Social Order*. Leyden, 1959.
Council of Europe. *Handbook of European Organizations*. Strasbourg, 1956.
——. *Notre Europe*. Strasbourg, 1958.
Deutsch, Karl W., and others. *Political Community and the North Atlantic Area*. Princeton, 1957.
Dewhurst, J. Frederic, and others. *Europe's Needs and Resources*. New York, 1961.
Diebold, William, Jr. "Theory and Practice of European Integration." *World Politics*, Vol. XI, No. 4 (July, 1959), pp. 621–28.
Documentation Française, La. *L'Organisation de L'Europe Occidentale*. (*Notes et Etudes Documentaires, Série internationale* CCCXX ff.). Paris, 1955.
European Cultural Centre. *Les Origines de L'Europe. Bulletin du Centre Européen de la Culture*. 7e Année, No. 1, March, 1959.
European Movement. *European American Survey*. Brussels, 1957.
European Yearbook. Annual, The Hague.
Florinsky, Michael T. *Integrated Europe?* New York, 1955.
Fontaine, François. *La nation frein*. Paris, 1956.
Foreign Policy Association—World Affairs Center. "Focus on Regional Organizations." *Intercom*, Vol. II, No. 8 (December, 1960).
Freeman, Alwyn V. "The Development of International Co-operation in the Peaceful Use of Atomic Energy." *American Journal of International Law*, Vol. LIV, No. 2 (April, 1960), pp. 383–92.
van der Goes van Naters, Marinus. *Le développement de l'intégration économique de l'Europe*. Assemblée Commune de la C.E.C.A. Luxembourg, 1955.

Gordon, Lincoln. "Myth and Reality in European Integration." *Yale Review*, Vol. XLV, No. 1 (September, 1955), pp. 80–103.

——. "Nato and European Integration." *World Politics*, Vol. X, No. 2 (January, 1958), pp. 219–31.

Haas, Ernst B. "The Challenge of Regionalism." *International Organization*, Vol. XII, No. 4 (Autumn, 1958), pp. 440–58.

——. "Regionalism, Functionalism and Universal International Organization." *World Politics*, Vol. VIII, No. 2 (January, 1956), pp. 238–63.

——, and Merkl, Peter H. "Parliamentarians Against Ministers : the Case of Western European Union." *International Organization*, Vol. XIV, No. 1 (Winter, 1960), pp. 37–59.

Haines, C. Grove. "What Future for Europe?" *Headline Series*, No. 124 (July–August, 1957).

—— (ed.). *European Integration*. Baltimore, 1957.

Halecki, Oscar. *The Limits and Divisions of European History*. London, 1950.

Hartog, F. *European Trade Cycle Policy*. Leyden, 1959.

Haviland, H. Field, Jr. (ed.). *The United States and the Western Community*. Haverford, Penn., 1957.

Hay, Denys. *Europe: the Emergence of an Idea*. Edinburgh, 1957.

Hitchner, Dell G. "Supranational Organization and Democracy in Western Europe." *Parliamentary Affairs*, Vol. XI, No. 3 (Summer, 1958), pp. 273–86.

Jenks, C. Wilfred. "World Organization and European Integration." *European Yearbook*, Vol. I (1955), pp. 173–86.

Jennings, W. Iver. *A Federation of Western Europe*. London, 1940.

Kraft, Joseph. *The Grand Design: From Common Market and Atlantic Partnership*. New York, 1962.

Landheer, B. "Sociological Aspects of European Integration." *European Yearbook*, Vol. III (1957), pp. 53–67.

Lerner, Daniel and Aron, Raymond (eds.). *France Defeats E.D.C.* New York, 1957.

Lindsay, Kenneth. *European Assemblies*. New York, 1960.

Lippmann, Walter. *Western Unity and the Common Market*. Boston, 1962.

Looper, Robert B. "Federalism and European Economic Integration." *International Relations*, Vol. I, No. 7 (April, 1957), pp. 303–10.

Macmahon, Arthur W. (ed.). *Federalism: Mature and Emergent*. New York, 1955.

Marc, Alexandre. *L'Europe, terre decisive*. Paris, 1959.

Massip, Roger. *Voici L'Europe*. Paris, 1958.

Meade, James E. Negotiations for Benelux: an Annotated Chronicle. Princeton, 1957.

Monnet, Jean. *Les Etats-Unis d'Europe ont Commencé*. Paris, 1955.

Moore, Ben. *Nato and the Future of Europe*. New York, 1958.

National Industrial Conference Board. *Economic Unity in Europe.* New York, 1960.

Nelson, George R. "European Organisation in the Field of Atomic Energy." *European Yearbook*, Vol. IV (1958), pp. 36–58.

Northrop, F. S. C. *European Union and United States Foreign Policy*. New York, 1954.

Political and Economic Planning. *European Organisations*. London, 1959.

——. *Atlantic Tariffs and Trade*. London, 1962.

Racine, Raymond (ed.). *Demain l'Europe Sans Frontières?* Paris, 1958.

Robertson, A. H. *European Institutions*. New York, 1959.

Sannwald, Rolf, and Stohler, Jacques. *Wirtschaftliche Integration*. Basel/Tübingen, 1958.

Scitovsky, Tibor. *Economic Theory and Western European Integration*. London, 1958.

Stadler, K. R. *Adult Education and European Co-operation*. Leyden, 1960.

Trempont, Jacques. *L'Unification de L'Europe*. Amiens/Brussels, 1955.

Triffin, Robert. *Europe and the Money Muddle*. New Haven, Conn., 1957.

Voyenne, Bernard. *Petite Histoire de L'Idée Européenne*. Paris, 1954.

Yalem, Ronald J. "Prospects for European Political Unification." *Western Political Quarterly,* Vol. XII, No. 1 (March, 1959), pp. 50–63.

Zurcher, Arnold J. *The Struggle to Unite Europe, 1940–1958*. New York, 1958.

THE EUROPEAN COMMUNITY

Bailey, Richard. *L'Intégration Economique en Europe*. Turin, 1960.

Bebr, Gerhard. "The Balance of Power in the European Communities." *European Yearbook*, Vol. V (1959), pp. 53–75.

Bonacina, Franco. *L'Europa diventa un Fatto*. Rome, 1960.

Compagna, Francesco (ed.). *Gli anni difficili della Comunità Europea*. Special number of *Nord e Sud*, N.S. Anno VII, Nos. 11–12 (December, 1960).

Federal Bar Association. *Institute on Legal Aspects of the European Community*. Washington, 1960.

Gerbet, Pierre. *La France et l'organisation de l'Europe*. Paris, n.d.

Ginestet, Pierre. *L'Assemblée Parlementaire Européenne*. Paris, 1959.

Hallstein, Walter. *United Europe — Challenge and Opportunity*. Cambridge, Mass., 1962.

Heidelberg, Franz C. *Das Europäische Parlament*. Baden-Baden/Bonn/Frankfurt am Main, 1959.

Heilbroner, Robert L. *Forging a United Europe: the Story of the European Community*. New York, 1961.

Kroebel, Gerhard, and others. *Die Europäische Integration*. Düsseldorf, 1961.

Lapie, Pierre-Olivier. *Les trois communautés*. Paris, 1960.

Legal Problems of the E.E.C. and the E.F.T.A. Report of a conference held in London in September 1960. London, 1961.

Meade, J. E., Liesner, H. H., Wells, S. J. *Case Studies on European Economic Union*. Oxford, 1962.

Mikesell, Raymond F. "The Lessons of Benelux and the European Coal and Steel Community for the European Economic Community." *American Economic Review*, Vol. XLVIII, No. 2 (May, 1958), pp. 428-41.

Political and Economic Planning. *Direct Elections and the European Parliament*. Occasional Paper No. 10. London, 1960.

———. *France and the European Community*. Occasional Paper No. 11. London, 1961.

———. *The Negotiations on Political Union. Planning*. Vol. XXVIII, No. 465, London, 1962.

Pryce, Roy. *The Political Future of the European Community*. London, 1962.

Rideau, Emile. *Euratom, Marché Commun et C.E.C.A.: Bilan, espoirs et risques*. Paris, 1957.

Romus, Paul. *Expansion économique régionale et Communauté Européenne*. Leyden, 1958.

E.C.S.C.

Bailey, Richard. "The European Coal and Steel Community, 1952 to 1956." *The British Survey*, N.S. No. 83 (February, 1956), pp. 13-24.

Bebr, Gerhard. "The Development of a Community Law by the Court of the European Coal and Steel Community." *Minnesota Law Review*, Vol. CXLII, No. 5 (April, 1958), pp. 845-78.

——. "Labor and the Schuman Plan." *Michigan Law Review*, Vol. LII, No. 7 (May, 1954), pp. 1007–22.

——. "Protection of Private Interests under the European Coal and Steel Community." *Virginia Law Review*, Vol. XLII, No. 7 (November, 1956), pp. 879–925.

——. "The Relation of the E.C.S.C. Law to the Law of the Member States." *Columbia Law Review*, Vol. LVIII, No. 6 (June, 1958), pp. 767–97.

Blondeel, Jean L., and Vander Eycken, Henri. "Les Emprunts de la Communauté Européenne du Charbon et de l'Acier." *Revue de la Banque*, 10e Année, Nos. 3–4 (1955), pp. 250–287.

De Soto, Jean. *La C.E.C.A.* Paris, 1958.

Diebold, William, Jr. *The Schuman Plan*. New York, 1959.

Gerbet, Pierre. "La Genèse du Plan Schuman." *Revue Française de Science Politique*, Vol. VI, No. 3 (1956), pp. 525–53.

Goormaghtigh, John. "European Coal and Steel Community." *International Conciliation*, No. 503 (May, 1955), pp. 343–408.

Haas, Ernst B. *The Uniting of Europe*. London, 1958.

Lang, Norbert. "Trade Regulations in the Treaty establishing the European Coal and Steel Community." *Northwestern University Law Review*, Vol. LII, No. 8 (June, 1958), pp. 1079–1116.

Lister, Louis. *Europe's Coal and Steel Community*. New York, 1960.

Mason, Henry L. *The European Coal and Steel Community*. The Hague, 1955.

Mathijsen, Pierre. *Le Droit de la Communauté Européenne du Charbon et de l'Acier*. The Hague, 1958.

Merry, Henry J. "The European Coal and Steel Community—Operations of the High Authority." *Western Political Quarterly*, Vol. VIII, No. 2 (June,1955), pp. 166–185.

Peeters, Marcel. "La C.E.C.A. et les nouvelles perspectives économiques en Europe." *La Vie Economique et Sociale*, 28e Année, Nos. 1–2 (1957), pp. 1–27.

Root, Franklin R. *The European Coal and Steel Community*. Studies in Business and Economics Vol. IX, No. 3 (December, 1955) and Vol. X, No. 1 (June, 1956). Maryland.

Sanderson, Fred H. "The Five-Year Experience of the European Coal and Steel Community." *International Organization*, Vol. XII, No. 2 (Spring, 1958), pp. 193–200.

Stein, Eric. "The Court of Justice of the European Coal and Steel Community: 1954–1957." *American Journal of International Law*, Vol. LI, No. 4 (October, 1957), pp. 821–9.

——. "The European Coal and Steel Community: the Beginnings of its Judicial Process." *Columbia Law Review*, Vol. LV, No. 7 (November, 1955), pp. 985–99.

Valentine, Donald G. *The Court of Justice and the European Coal and Steel Community.* The Hague, 1954.

——. "The First Judgements of the Court of Justice of the European Coal and Steel Community." *Modern Law Review,* Vol. XX, No. 6 (November, 1957), pp. 596–619.

Van Houtte, Albert. "La Cour de Justice de la Communauté Européenne du Charbon et de l'Acier." *European Yearbook,* Vol. II (1956), pp. 183–222.

Vernon, Raymond. "The Schuman Plan : Sovereign Powers of the European Coal and Steel Community." *American Journal of International Law,* Vol. XLVII, No. 2 (April, 1953), pp. 183–202.

Williams, Shirley. *The Common Market and its Forerunners.* Fabian Research Series No. 201. London, October, 1958.

EURATOM

Errera, Jacques, and others. *Euratom, analyses et commentaires.* Brussels, 1958.

Gaudet, Michel. "Euratom." *Progress in Nuclear Energy,* Series 10, Vols. 1 and 2—Law and Administration (New York, 1959), pp. 140–79.

Hahn, Hugo J. "Control under the Euratom Compact." *American Journal of Comparative Law,* Vol. VII, No. 1 (Winter, 1958), pp. 23–46.

——. "Euratom : the Concept of an International Personality." *Harvard Law Review,* Vol. LXXI, No. 6 (April, 1958), pp. 1001–56.

Johnson, James G., Jr. "An Introduction to the European Atomic Energy Community (Euratom)." *Business Lawyer,* Vol. XIII, No. 4 (July, 1958). pp. 801–12.

Kohnstamm, Max. "Europe and Atoms for Power." *Atoms for Power,* New York, pp. 140–9.

Knorr, Klaus E. *Euratom and American Policy.* Princeton, 1956.

Mayne, Richard. "Euratom." *The Rotarian,* Vol. XCIII, No. 7 October, 1958), pp. 8–60.

Moore, Ben T. *Euratom: the American Interest in the European Atomic Energy Community.* New York, 1958.

Rieben, Henri. "Euratom." *Revue économique et sociale,* Lausanne, January, 1957.

COMMON MARKET

Albertini, J. -M., and others. *Du Marché Commun à une Politique Européenne.* Paris, 1959.

Allen, James Jay. *The European Common Market and the G.A.T.T.* Washington, 1960.

Association des Universitaires d'Europe. *Marché Commun: Institutions Communes.* Paris, 1960.

Association of British Chambers of Commerce. *Aids to Investment in the European Economic Community.* London, 1960.

——. *Index to the Treaty of Rome.* London, 1961.

Association of the Bar of the City of New York, Committee on Foreign Law. "The European Economic Community : some Problems for Consideration by Lawyers." *The Record,* Vol. XIV, No. 7 (October, 1959), pp. 365–90.

Bowie, Robert R., and Geiger, Theodore. *The European Economic Community and the United States.* Washington, U.S. Printing Office, 1961.

British Institute of International and Comparative Law. *Legal Problems of the European Economic Community and the European Free Trade Association.* London, 1961.

Business International. *Europe's Mass Markets.* New York, 1960.

Cabot, Thomas D. *Common Market: Economic Foundation for a U.S. of Europe?* New York, 1959.

Camps, Miriam. *The European Common Market and American Policy.* Princeton, 1956.

——. *The First Year of the European Economic Community.* Princeton, 1958.

Committee for Economic Development. *The European Common Market and its Meaning to the United States.* New York, 1959.

Daily Herald. *The Treaty of Rome.* London, 1961.

Delagneau, Bernard. *L'Association des pays d'outre-mer à la Communauté Economique Européenne.* Louvain, 1961.

Deniau, J.-F. *The Common Market.* London, 1960. 2nd ed. London, 1961.

Dixon, Roger C. "European Policies on Restrictive Business Practices." *American Economic Review,* Vol. XLVIII, No. 2 (May, 1958), pp. 442–51.

Documentation Française, La. *Le Marché Commun.* (Notes et Etudes Documentaires, Série économique et financière DC.). Paris, 1960.

Editions du Monde Ouvrier. *Le Marché Commun: chômage ou prosperité?* Paris, 1959.

Efron, Reuben, and Nanes, Allan S. "The Common Market and Euratom Treaties : Supranationality and the Integration of Europe." *International and Comparative Law Quarterly,* Vol. VI, No. 4 (October, 1957), pp. 670–84.

European Cultural Centre. *Promesses du Marché Commun. Bulletin du Centre Européen de la Culture*, 5e Année, No. 6, December, 1957.

European League for Economic Co-operation. *European Investment Bank Problems.* Brussels, 1960.

Félice, Pierre de. *Le Marché Commun Agricole.* 2nd ed. Paris, n.d.

Frank, Isaiah. *The European Common Market: An Analysis of Commercial Policy.* New York, 1961.

Fry, Richard. *The Common Market in Action.* London, 1960.

Gather, Gernot, and others. *Gemeinsamer Markt. Offene Welt*, No. 62. Cologne/Opladen, 1959.

Gehrels, Franz. "Monetary Systems for the Common Market." *Journal of Finance*, Vol. XIV, No. 2 (May, 1959), pp. 312–21.

Gehrels, Franz, and Johnston, Bruce F. "The Economic Gains of European Integration." *Journal of Political Economy*, Vol. LXIII, No. 4 (August, 1955), pp. 275–92.

Giordano, Renato. *Il Mercato Comune e i suoi problemi.* Rome, 1958.

Hunt, James. *Europe and Africa—can it be partnership?* London, n.d.

Hurtig, Serge. "The European Common Market." *International Conciliation*, No. 517 (March, 1958), pp. 321–81.

Krassa, Lucie G. *The European Economic Community.* Studies in Business and Economics Vol. XIII, No. 2 (September, 1959) and No. 3 (December, 1959). Maryland.

Lojewski, Werner von. *Der Gemeinsame Markt in Europa.* Frankfurt am Main, 1958.

Mahotière, Stuart de la. *The Common Market.* London, 1961.

Malvestiti, Piero. *Pourquoi le Marché Commun.* Milan, 1958.

Marjolin, Robert. "Prospects for the European Common Market." *Foreign Affairs*, Vol. XXXVI, No. 1 (October, 1957), pp. 131–42.

Marting, Elizabeth (ed.). *The European Common Market: New Frontier for American Business.* New York, 1958.

Minet, Paul. *Full Text of the Rome Treaty and an A.B.C. of the Common Market.* London, 1961.

Niehaus, Heinrich. "Effects of the European Common Market on Employment and Social Conditions in Agriculture." *International Labour Review*, Vol. LXXVII, No. 4 (April, 1958), pp. 289–312.

Nortcliffe, E. B. *Common Market Fiscal Systems.* London, 1960.

Pinay, Antoine, and others. "Le Marché Commun." *Revue Politique et Parlementaire*, 60e Année, No. 685 (December, 1958), pp. 419–69.

Political and Economic Planning. *Agricultural Policy in the European Economic Community*. Occasional Paper No. 1. London, 1958.

——. *Budgetary Control in the European Economic Community*. Occasional Paper No. 6. London, 1960.

——. *Cartel Policy and the Common Market*. Planning. Vol. XXVIII, No. 464, London, 1962.

——. *Proposals for a Common Agricultural Policy in E.E.C.* Occasional Paper No. 5. London, 1960.

——. *Trade Unions and the Common Market*. Planning. Vol. XXVIII, No. 461, London, 1962.

Rueff, Jacques. *Le projet de communauté économique européenne.* Turin, 1957.

Rueff, Jacques, and others. *Le Marché Commun et ses problémes.* Paris, 1958.

Stein, Eric. "An Emergent Legal Community: the Common Market Countries' Plans for Harmonization of Law." *American Journal of Comparative Law*, Vol. IX, No. 2 (Spring, 1960), pp. 351–8.

Stein, Eric, and Nicholson, Thomas L. *American Enterprise in the European Common Market: a Legal Profile.* Ann Arbor, 1960.

Strauss, E. *Common Sense about the Common Market.* London, 1958.

Times, The. *The Common Market*. London, 1961.

Tinbergen, Jan. *The European Community and the Underdeveloped Countries.* Paris, 1959. (Mimeographed.)

Uri, Pierre, and others. "L'Intégration européenne." *Revue Economique*. No. 2 (March, 1958), pp. 169–312.

Walton, Clarence C. "Implications of the European Common Market on Member and Non-Member States." *Duquesne Review*, Vol. IV, No. 1 (Fall, 1958), pp. 30–44.

Whitlow, Robert S. "The European Economic Community : some aspects of juridical personality, sovereignty and international obligation." *Business Lawyer*, Vol. XIII, No. 4 (July, 1958), pp. 813–30.

Wilberforce, R. O. "Restrictive Trade Practices in the European Common Market." *Journal of Business Law*, April, 1958, pp. 120–30.

Yaeger, Leland B. "Exchange rates within a common market." *Social Research*, Vol. XXV, No. 4 (Winter, 1958), pp. 415–38.

BRITAIN AND EUROPE, F.T.A., E.F.T.A., etc.

Allen, H. C. *The Anglo-American Predicament.* London, 1960.

Anouil, Gilles. *La Grande-Bretagne et la Communauté Européenne du Charbon et de l'Acier.* Issoudun, 1960.

A.B.C. Weekend Television. *Will Farmers Suffer if Britain Joins the Common Market?* London, 1961.

Association of British Chambers of Commerce, Federation of British Industries, National Union of Manufacturers. *A Joint Report on the European Free Trade Area.* London, 1957.

Bareau, Paul. *Europe: The Next Steps.* London, 1957.

Beloff, Max. *New Dimensions in Foreign Policy.* London, 1961.

Benoit, Emile. *Europe at Sixes and Sevens.* New York, 1961.

Brown, Michael Barratt, and Hughes, John. *Britain's Crisis and the Common Market.* London, 1961.

Camps, Miriam. *Division in Europe.* Political and Economic Planning Occasional Paper No. 8. London, 1960.

——. *The European Common Market and Free Trade Area: a Progress Report.* Princeton, 1957.

——. *The European Free Trade Association: a Preliminary Appraisal.* Political and Economic Planning Occasional Paper No. 4. London, 1959.

——. *Four Approaches to the European Problem.* Political and Economic Planning Occasional Paper No. 12. London, 1961.

——. *The Free Trade Area Negotiations.* Political and Economic Planning Occasional Paper No. 2. London, 1959.

Carrington, C. E. (ed.) "The European Economic Community and the Commonwealth." *Western World*, Vol. III, No. 2 (February, 1960).

Council of Europe. *The Position of Certain European Countries other than the Six in the event of the United Kingdom joining the European Economic Community.* Strasbourg, 1961.

Daily Express. *You and the Common Market.* London, 1961.

Daily Mirror. *Britain and Europe.* London, 1961.

Daily Telegraph. *Britain and the Common Market.* London, 1961.

Driscoll, James. *Britain and the European Market.* London, 1956.

Economist Intelligence Unit. *Britain, the Commonwealth, and European Free Trade.* London, 1958.

——. *Britain and Europe.* London, 1957.

——. *The Commonwealth and Europe.* London, 1960.

——. *If Britains Joins.* London, 1961.

Federal Educational and Research Trust. *Britain in Europe.* London, 1957.

Federal Trust for Education and Research. *The Commonwealth and Europe.* London, 1960.

Federal Union. Britain, Europe, and the Commonwealth. London, 1958. (Mimeographed.)

Federation of British Industry. *British Industry and Europe.* London, 1961.

————. *European Free Trade Area*. London, 1957.

Grimond, Jo, and others. *Britain Must Join*. New Directions, No. 1.

Hallett, Graham. *British Agriculture and Europe*. London, 1961.

Heiser, H. J. *British Policy with Regard to the Unification Efforts on the European Continent*. Leyden, 1959.

Huizinga, J. H. *Confessions of a European in England*. London, 1958.

Industrial Federations and Employers' Organizations of Austria, Denmark, Norway, Sweden, Switzerland, and the United Kingdom. *Free Trade in Western Europe*. Paris, 1948.

Institute of International Finance. *The Common Market and Free Trade Area*. Bulletin No. 206. New York, 1958.

Kitzinger, U. W. *The Challenge of the Common Market*. Oxford, 1961.

————. "Europe : the Six and the Seven." *International Organization*, Vol. XIV, No. 1. (Winter, 1960), pp. 20–36.

Kreinin, Mordechai E. "The 'Outer-Seven' and European Integration." *American Economic Review*, Vol. L, No. 3 (June, 1960), pp. 370–86.

Lamb, Richard. *The Future of Farming and Food Prices in the Common Market*. Policy document of the Farmers' and Smallholders' Association. London, 1961.

Layton, Christopher. *Britain's European Dilemma*. London, n.d.

Lewis, Russell, and Morris, Anthony F. C. *Challenge from Europe*. London, 1957.

Luard, Evan. *Britain and Europe*. London, 1961.

Meade, James E. "The Balance-of-Payments Problems of a European Free Trade Area." *Economic Journal*, Vol. LXVII, No. 267 (September, 1957), pp. 376–96.

————. UK, Commonwealth and Common Market (Hobart Paper 17). London, 1962.

Meyer, F. V. *The Seven*. London, 1960.

National Farmers' Association (Ireland). *The Common Market and the Irish Farmer*. Dublin, 1961.

National Farmers' Union. *Agriculture in the Community*. London, 1961.

————. *British Agriculture and the Common Market*. London, 1961.

Nevin, Edward. *Wales and the Common Market*. Carmarthen, 1960.

Nutting, Anthony. *Europe Will Not Wait*. London, 1960.

Payne, Lewis, and Wills, R. L. *The Seven*. London, n.d.

Pickles, William. *Not With Europe: the political case for staying out*. London, 1962.

Pig Industry Development Authority. *Pigs and the Common Market*. London, 1961.

Pinder, John. *Britain and the Common Market*. London, 1961.

Piquet, Howard S. *The European Free Trade Association: Implications for U.S. Exports*. New York, 1960.

Political and Economic Planning. *Agriculture, the Commonwealth, and E.E.C.* Occasional Paper No. 14. London, 1961.

——. *Commonwealth Preference in the United Kingdom*. London, 1960.

——. *Food Prices and the Common Market*. Occasional Paper No. 13. London, 1961.

——. *Problems of Freer Trade in Europe*. Planning, Vol. XXIV, No. 423. London, 1958.

——. *Tariffs and Trade in Western Europe*. London, 1959.

——. *Trade Diversion in Western Europe*. Occasional Paper No. 9. London, 1960.

Royal Institute of International Affairs. *Britain in Western Europe*. London/New York, 1956.

Scott, M. F. G. "Britain, the Commonwealth, and Europe." Bulletin of the Oxford Institute of Statistics, Vol. XXIII, No. 1. (February, 1961), pp. 27–47.

Siegler, Heinrich. *Dokumentation der Europäischen Integration. 1946–1961 mit besonderer Berücksichtigung des Verhältnisses EWG–EFTA*. Bonn/Vienna/Zürich, 1961.

Soper, Tom (ed.) *Europe and the Commonwealth*. London, 1960.

Stranner, Henri. *Neutralité Suisse et Solidarité Européenne*. 2nd ed. Lausanne, 1960.

Trades Union Congress. *Economic Association with Europe*. London, 1956.

United Kingdom Council of the European Movement. *Britain's Food and the Common Market*. London, 1961.

University of London Department of Extra-Mural Studies and the Institute of Bankers. *The European Common Market and Free Trade Area*. London, 1958.

Warley, T. K. *The Impact of European Economic Integration on British Agriculture and the Commonwealth*. Nottingham, 1961.

Westminster Bank Limited. *The Common Market and the United Kingdom*. London, 1961.

Williams, Shirley. *Britain and the Free Trade Area*. London, 1958.

Worswick, G. D. N. "Britain, the Common Market and a Free Trade Area." *Year Book of World Affairs*, Vol. XII (1958), pp. 181–98.

——. (ed.) *The Free Trade Area Proposals*. Oxford, 1960.

References to governmental and Community publications, which are not included in the above selection, will be found in the compilations listed under the heading *BIBLIOGRAPHIES*.

INDEX